"We can teach the gospel without it reaching us because we feel the need to prove our sufficiency in order to justify our leadership in the church. Barbara Bancroft urges us to live beyond the clichés we impose on ourselves in order to live in the freedom of the gospel that will set free the women and men we lead."

Bryan and Kathy Chapell, Authors of *Each for the Other: Marriage as It's Meant to Be*; ministering at Grace Presbyterian Church in Peoria, IL

"Thank you, Barbara, for taking the time to write to us. You identify the struggles of women in ministry and point us to the Truth. Even for women who have studied Scripture, you make this book fresh and hopeful. To be comfortable in our own skin because of Jesus—yes, it is possible."

Ed and Sheri Welch, Author; faculty member at the Christian Counseling & Educational Foundation (Ed); administrator at Bridge Community Church, Glenside, PA (Sheri)

"Barbara Bancroft has been a longtime friend and fellow worker in God's vineyard. Both of us have learned much about our weakness and God's astonishing gospel to help us navigate through the pitfalls of life and ministry. She is passionate about her need and the need of the women to whom she is writing to stand firm in the truth when we are tempted to get sidelined by our sin, or the sins of others. She is also very honest about her own weaknesses and failures, but knows there is no help outside of going to Christ daily for forgiveness, and to trust again in the power of the Spirit to continue to reach out to a needy and broken world."

Rose Marie Miller, Missionary to London; author of *From Fear to Freedom* and *Nothing Is Impossible with God*

"Let's go ahead and cut to the chase—*Running on Empty* is simply the **best** book Darlene and I have ever read on the 'raptures and ruptures' of vocational ministry, and the radical implications of God's grace for wives and women who are seeking to serve Jesus. As an adjunct faculty member of five seminaries, I will now require this book, not only for the women in my classes, but for every man who is presently or plans to get married; for men need to understand, not just the privileges of ministry, but also the setups and heartaches women face—things they 'didn't sign on for.' Darlene and I got married in 1972 and never thought we would wear the couple title, 'pastor and pastor's wife,' and nothing could have prepared us for the delights and demands, and dissolution and despair ahead. Barbara's book would have been a gift of invaluable benefit to us, not only as we began our ministry, but through every stage of our shared life. Filled with gospel wisdom and personal anecdotes, beautiful honesty and the hope of grace, Barbara throws the spotlight on Jesus's love and the freedom he intends for all of us who are passionate to serve him."

Scotty and Darlene Smith, Ministering at West End Community Church, Nashville, TN; formerly ministering at Christ Community Church, Franklin, TN

"Women in ministry face unique challenges and this book is uniquely helpful. It offers real hope to women who are worn down by the demands of ministry—hope based on the good news that Jesus has paid it all and done it all. After I read this book, this old pastor's wife felt encouraged and strengthened by the good news of who Christ is and what he has done for me and those I serve. If it could help me, it will help anyone!"

Barbara Miller Juliani, Pastor's wife; author; editor

"I'm not a fan of Christian books, so I was surprised to discover laughter and tears as I read *Running on Empty*. With a rare economy of words, Barbara pinpoints the rumblings of our soul, names the unidentified issues, and compassionately takes us to the one place we can be filled. If you're a woman in ministry, work with one, or know one, this book is for you."

Shari Thomas, Founder/Director of Parakaleo

"Please don't buy this book . . . unless you want real help for real women in real ministry. Barbara Bancroft has that rare blend of rich ministry experience without the accompanying cynicism or Pollyanna-like attitude that affects so many of us. Instead, she offers us a voice that whispers behind us, 'This is the way. Walk in it.' Barbara Bancroft doesn't tackle all of the exegetical conundrums of Scripture in relation to women. She doesn't intend to. Rather, she elucidates and, with humor and humility, illustrates sound principles of gospel application which have been proven in a variety of cultural contexts. I'm thankful for this book. It will help not just women in ministry, but ministry marriages like mine."

John F. Thomas, Director of Global Training, Redeemer City to City

"In *Running on Empty*, Barbara Bancroft utilizes personal insight and transparent humility to highlight topics of interest for women in ministry. Whether co-laboring with a husband or single, women in ministry often do not know what they do not know. Barbara sheds light on this for all of us. With captivating stories and heart-probing questions, she helps women navigate issues like entitlement, comparison, worry, and self-pity. Her words are comforting and encouraging. While reading, I felt as if I could have been sitting in Barbara's living room, sipping tea, listening to her tell her story, and soaking up her wisdom."

Daniel and Mandy Montgomery, Ministering at Sojourn Community Church, Louisville, KY

"Barbara's remarkable book will help you answer many hard questions: If I do marry a pastor, what will my life be like? If I am already a pastor's wife, what do I need to remember about Jesus to survive? But much more basic and blessed for all of us, is that deepest issue of all: how do I put together the blessedness of Jesus in my life with all the hard things that threaten my faith? This book is honest and genuine, and points directly to Jesus in many unexpected deep ways."

D. Clair Davis, Professor of Church History Emeritus, Westminster Theological Seminary

"Barbara is the real deal. She doesn't just give advice on ministry; she invites you into the journey with her toward the overflowing pool of reliance and nourishment that is God's Word. Barbara's book is full of gutsy grace and loving transparency . . . we wish we'd had the courage to write it."

Rev. Dr. Stephen and Berenice Rarig, Church Planting Team Leader, Mission To The World; cofounder Trinity Theological College, Perth Western Australia (Stephen); Founder, Coordinator MAKE Collective (Berenice)

Running on Empty
The Gospel for Women in Ministry

Barbara Bancroft

New
Growth
Press

www.newgrowthpress.com

New Growth Press, Greensboro, NC 27404
Copyright © 2014 Barbara Bancroft

Cover Design: Faceout Books, faceout.com
Interior Design and Typesetting: Lisa Parnell, lparnell.com

ISBN 978-1-939946-35-5 (Print)
ISBN 978-1-939946-36-2 (eBook)

Library of Congress Cataloging-in-Publication Data
Bancroft, Barbara, 1955–
  Running on empty : the gospel for women in ministry / Barbara
Bancroft.
    pages cm
  ISBN 978-1-939946-35-5 (alk. paper)
  1. Women in church work. I. Title.
  BV4415.B25 2014
  253.082—dc23

                                                        2013041750

Printed in USA

21 20 19 18 17 16 15   2 3 4 5

DEDICATION

For my sweetheart, Josiah, who keeps life interesting.

Contents

Acknowledgments

I owe a huge debt of gratitude to all of the women in ministry who have given me access to their struggles and successes. You know who you are. A very special thanks to my son, Josiah V, a published writer and gifted teacher whose patient tutorials on grammar, insightful comments, and support for the project were invaluable. A heartfelt thanks goes to my dear family, whom I ignored on many occasions to meet a deadline. Your support was an ongoing encouragement. And lastly, this book would not have been written without my husband's willingness to explore the world of frozen dinners, answer random theological questions, and endure a wife who was often lost in thought. Thanks, Josiah.

Chapter 1

Are You Ready
For Some Ministry?

Ready: prepared for immediate action or use; inclined;
apt to happen; liable at any moment. (Wiktionary)

IN THE LATE 1970s, my husband, Josiah, and I spent his seminary internship in a sunny Florida city. A regular part of Josiah's responsibilities was to take care of all who came to the church seeking help. One afternoon he arrived at our apartment with a homeless man, a paranoid schizophrenic who needed a shower, clean clothes, and dinner. The shower, clean clothes, and dinner I could understand, but what I found hard to fathom was that Josiah brought this fellow home—to his pregnant wife and two preschool children—to provide them. The dinner conversation that evening was as odd as you might imagine. And later, it took lots of scrubbing before I could put our children back in the bathtub our guest had used for his shower. I knew Christ wanted me to love troubled souls like this man, but I was not happy that Josiah had brought this particular troubled soul home for me to love. I resented Josiah for what he had done and my faith faltered. My resentment was quickly followed by shame at my response to such a small request

1

for kindness. The weakness of my faith was revealed as I lost my connection with God's desire to use me in our corner of the world.

Since then, Josiah and I have learned a lot through our years in ministry. Josiah has learned that I respond better if I have some lead time before a difficult situation. I have learned that I have to be ready for ministry *before* the moment arrives.

What *is* ministry? Ministry is our daily answer to Christ's call to love the world and communicate his good news. The unexpectedness of what we are sometimes asked to do exposes our inadequacies, as the visit from the homeless man exposed mine. Those moments often catch us at our most vulnerable (in my case, pregnant and exhausted by preschoolers) to highlight how truly needy we are. I thought of myself as hospitable and loving until this troubled man exposed the tenuous nature of my hospitality and love.

When ministry pushes us to do things we do not want to do, we may feel alone and inadequate or resentful and rebellious. When things get hard, the first question that often comes to mind is, "Where are you, Lord?" We assume that Jesus has left us on our own to feel the poverty of our resources. If you have ever found yourself inadequate for the task at hand or unable to love the people who come your way, you know what I mean. Ministry confronts us with our insufficiency over and over. I have learned that I am better able to respond with faith if I am ready for these moments *before* they occur. So, how do we ready ourselves for ministry?

I have written this book for women whose vocation is Christian ministry, whether we work alongside a husband or pursue our own ministry. Although, every child of God is involved in ministry as part of their identity and calling, I have a heart for women facing the special challenges of vocational ministry. Many of us are running on empty as people and obligations press in. I am persuaded that, more than anything else the good news of Christ's coming is the good news that *we* need to hear *for ourselves*. The gospel message is not just information we share with others; our personal encounter with the promises of the gospel is what readies *us* for ministry and fills *our tanks*. Knowing that our sins are forgiven, that we stand in Christ's righteousness this and every day, and that he will use us for his kingdom work is our ministry preparation. In this book, I will tell you how the gospel is changing me, and offer hope that it will also change you.

The changes God works in us to ready us for ministry may not be what others expect, but Jesus never calls us to fulfill the stereotypes and expectations others have of us. We can stop using them to evaluate ourselves, grade our progress, and assess our worth to the cause. His plans for us are deeper and broader than our truncated stereotypes. He calls each of us into a relationship with him. Our ability to satisfy expectations and stereotypes is a weak substitute for a relationship with Christ with some reality and life to it. Whether we minister alongside husbands or as single women, effective ministry will flow from us as Jesus grounds us in his love and the righteous life he purchased for us. I hope this book will give you a fresh look at how our relationship with Christ can change the way we experience and engage in ministry.

When Josiah and I began ministry life, I understood little of what I will share with you. I thought I understood the gospel and that what I lacked was formal training, abilities, and experience. Because I finished only one year at university and never had formal ministry training beyond a few seminary courses, I always felt the need to prove my worth. While I worked hard to fulfill the expectations of others, the inward pressure I placed on myself for a perfect ministry performance resulted in a chronic sense of failure and shame. The burden of seeking the good opinion of God and those around me was heavy, and I often stumbled under its weight. No matter what I did, it was never enough. My insecurities and self-dependence got in the way of the gospel's power to work in me.

I know the consequences of the weaknesses and sins that I brought into ministry, but I have also learned something from women who by temperament and training were more prepared for ministry than I was. Although God regularly uses people who are educated, trained, and experienced to move his kingdom forward, those whose confidence is in their abilities and experience can easily forget their need for Christ in the everyday of ministry. If we rarely question our abilities, it is tempting to rely on them to accomplish our goals instead of relying on the Spirit to work through us. We may live as if God's kingdom moves forward through our plans and efforts. Perhaps we accomplish more, but this can blind us to our pride and leave others with our competence as their model for spirituality. In short, whether we see ourselves as successes or failures in ministry, we will not be ready to do the work God has prepared for us to do until we know how to rely on nothing but the finished work of Christ.

Like many I have met in ministry, I have always had a noisy conscience. For years I felt guilt for what I deemed my feeble ministry efforts. This robbed me of the joy of being part of Christ's kingdom work. Thankfully, the burden of seeking others' approval has lightened as I have experienced God's approval, purchased for me on the cross, and his willingness to use me. I can't say that I never worry about what others think of me, but I can say that my need for their approval has diminished significantly over the years. You and I are no longer burdened to seek the approval of others. The gospel readies us for ministry by giving us confidence in God's approval each day.

As the gospel works its way into our lives, our focus shifts from the quality of our performance to the person of Christ. Turning to Christ in faith reorients us to the truth about what his work for us has accomplished. This in turn frees us from the burden of others' expectations and the weight of unhelpful pride in our achievements. Christ brings his good news to *our* hearts. We belong to him. He is the one who called us into ministry. He understands the struggles we face and the weariness we feel. He knows when we are misunderstood and underestimated. He knows what we fear. He knows our propensity for pride. He knows that ministry life can be confusing and chaotic. He knows we need some space to be ourselves. He knows our hearts become easily hardened as we fight to survive the pressures of ministry. He sees us hold back when we are certain we have nothing left to give. He would have given me the grace I needed to host our schizophrenic guest with a glad heart if I had simply asked him. He is the powerful Christ! He can change a heart. Simply turning to Christ for the help and comfort we need in our insufficiency strengthens our faith because he *will* help and comfort us. As we learn to live more and more in his presence, our experience of his love and care deepens and we begin to see real change. A heart abiding in Christ is prepared for ministry when it comes.

Some of us think we are in ministry because of our husband's vocation or a friend's urging, some unusual circumstance or because we raised our hand in an emotional moment during an altar call. But Christ's call to ministry is always intentional. There are no accidental ministers. Whether we are single or married, working in a church, on a campus, or with a mission organization, Christ has chosen us to make his gospel known to the world. He made us for the ministry into which he called us.

I have been in ministry with Josiah for thirty-six years. When I said, "I do," to Josiah, I also said, "I do" to ministry. Josiah and ministry were a package deal! Of course, I had no idea at the time what I was signing up for, either in marriage or ministry. Neither marriage books nor ministry books prepared me for the real thing. I remember being surprised, for example, that Josiah could not fix things around the house like my dad could. I remember the first time I was reprimanded by a deacon for a shopping bag he saw in my house from a nice department store. We usually do not recognize our expectations until they are exposed. I thought that all husbands liked to fix things around the house, and I thought that surely deacons of all people would be supportive rather than critical of the pastor's family.

My willingness to stay married and to remain in ministry have both been in jeopardy at times. Over the years, I have spoken with many women in ministry and, when I have been able to assure them that I am a safe person to be honest with, they have echoed my experiences. Those of us who are married soon discover that ministry puts considerable pressure on our marriages. (You brought *who* home for dinner!) It complicates parenting. (There are reasons for the volumes written on the struggles of pastors' kids and missionary kids.) If they desire marriage, single women may find that ministry makes it virtually impossible to find a mate, as many men are intimidated by their competence and intimate relationship with Christ. (Not to mention the small pool of dating material in many of the places women serve.) Ministry makes friendships more challenging. (How much can I confide? Whom can I trust?) Ministry pushes us into uncomfortable roles and awkward situations that do not fit us at all. (We all have examples here!) Regardless of our emotional response to Christ's call to ministry, his response to us is sure: "Before they call I will answer; while they are yet speaking I will hear" (Isaiah 65:24). He is quick to answer our prayers.

Although particulars differ, the strain of ministry is hard on both single and married women. During our first missionary term in the Republic of Ireland, we were privileged to have two single women on our team. Through their patient tutelage I began to understand some of the pressures they faced. Everything that is required to maintain life, single women do for themselves. In our family, I manage the bank account and Josiah manages the technology; I make the side dishes and he grills the meat. We divide our work. Yet single women do everything for themselves while working their demanding ministry jobs. To some they appear to have an abundance of free time. They can be viewed as convenient babysitters for missionary teams and church staffs.

Married women focus on the time and effort needed to nurture our marriages and children, but often forget that it takes an incredible amount of time and energy for single women to find and maintain relationships worth nurturing. I was recently with a single missionary whose roommate had returned to the States. She was filled with grief at the loss of this supportive friendship. Given the pressures involved in living where she did, she wondered if she had the emotional energy to invest in another relationship that she knew would be impermanent. Her faith challenge is to continue to invest herself in loving each roommate who enters her life, trusting that Jesus will care for her.

When I entered ministry as a pastor's wife, I did not understand the unique nature of Christ's call to me. I began ministry thinking that I was called to look like the mythically perfect pastors' wives I thought I knew. I did not realize that God's plan was to use my history, personality, gifts, passions, and abilities, mixed with Josiah's, to create a unique ministry that would change and grow as we did. Today it seems obvious to me that we would not be like anyone else and that God did not have a cookie-cutter ministry planned for us, but at the beginning of our ministry, we had both been taught to model ourselves after others. For many years this dynamic created tension in our marriage and ministry. Neither of us fit the molds we kept trying to squeeze ourselves (and each other) into. I wanted to give up on myself, marriage, and ministry many times because I was unable to be the woman I thought I was supposed to be. There were so many voices telling me what I should look like that I missed the reassuring voice of the Spirit, who was even then making me into the person Christ created me to be. It took a long time before I understood that Christ's plan was not to make me more like others but, rather, more like himself.

I have been a believer since I was nine years old. When I was ten, I knew God was calling me to be a missionary. When I was twenty, I married Josiah, who was on his way to seminary and the pastorate. I have spent eighteen years as a pastor's wife and eighteen years in missions. I have felt Christ's presence and love. You would think that faith would come more naturally to me because I have seen God answer countless prayers and do amazing things. Yet, after so many years of being in relationship with him and seeing him work, I still have doubts and fears. I still fall into cynicism and discouragement. There are times when my belief in his love wavers. There are times when I think he has made a mistake in choosing me for the job. But we will never step into ministry if we are waiting for perfect faith.

Josiah currently oversees the missionaries and stateside renewal ministries of Serge (formerly World Harvest Mission). We have traveled to many countries to work with missionary teams and nationals. We have logged thousands of miles in the U.S. meeting with pastors and their wives, speaking at conferences, recruiting for Serge teams, talking about how the gospel has changed us, and meeting with our financial and prayer supporters. Yet I rarely start a trip without some internal resistance. I am basically a homebody, hesitant around new people and unknown situations. My desire to follow Christ has not turned me into a different person. Still, Jesus gives me courage to say yes to opportunities when I want to say no. He makes me willing to board the plane when I want to stay home. My faith does not always feel in sync with his plan, yet the Spirit gets me where he wants me. He regularly answers my prayers for the grace I need for these trips, right when I need it. Although my faith is never perfect as I step into ministry, I have learned that if I step out with even the smallest amount of faith, he will supply what I lack. Christ's promise to his people is that he will be with us, provide what we need, and work through us. As we wake each morning, our job is to believe him. The power of Christ instills surprising faith in us at times, but even when our faith is weak, Christ will accomplish things through us. The quality and strength of our faith is not what matters, but that our faith rests only in him.

On one of our trips to India, Josiah and I split up for the second half of our visit. He was traveling with a missionary to explore a possible area of ministry in the northwest part of the country (a journey too dangerous for women at the time) while I was to travel from Delhi with the missionary's wife to her home (an eight-hour taxi ride). I would later have to make the eight-hour return trip by myself to meet Josiah before flying home to Ireland.

I was nervous about returning to Delhi alone. India is a big place with a lot of people. The day before we were to begin our separate journeys, I became violently ill. Josiah suggested that I check into a comfortable hotel to recover until he returned. What a tempting offer! After all, I was really sick. I did not have a lot of faith that day, but I had just enough to pray that if I was able to get out of bed and into the taxi the next morning, I would take that as God's answer to my fears of traveling alone. Sure enough, the next day although not well, I was able to get out of bed. I made the long trip with my friend that day settled in the knowledge that when it was time to return, God would give me the faith I needed.

I like to tell this story because it shows how God used my small mustard seed of faith to get me into a taxi. I know many brave missionary women, but I am not one of them. I could pretend that I am excited to find myself in strange places as I travel around the globe, but usually I find myself crying out for grace to navigate these new places. I do not want to miss the moments of ministry God provides because I am absorbed with worry about myself.

As we look to Scripture for insights into ministry life, we can find comfort and encouragement in the gospel's uncensored descriptions of the first disciples. We discover a lot by the way Jesus loved and tutored them through ministry. The New Testament did not catalog a group of holy men for us to emulate, but rather a group of ordinary men who struggled to believe. The disciples had all sorts of responses to Jesus and the situations he placed them in, and so do we. We read in Acts 1:6 that after all they had been through with Christ they were still confused about his plan of redemption. Jesus's plan to leave them behind was unexpected. How could they continue to follow him if he left them? They could no longer make sense of his call or his teaching.

Are you confused by God's thoughts and ways as he loves the world through you? The disciples were. His word of comfort to them was simple. He vowed never to leave them alone. He promised to send his Spirit to live in them. Jesus's word to us is the same. No matter how confusing things get, we are not alone as we take his good news to the world. He has sent his Spirit to live in us. Just as it was with his disciples, his answer to the confusion that ministry brings into our lives is to remind us that he has left us his Spirit. Whether the Spirit is convicting us of sin, comforting our hearts, or opening doors of ministry, his purpose is always to point us to the person and work of Christ. However the Spirit gets us to that moment, we will find Jesus waiting to receive us. This is the work of his Spirit.

The difficulty of an eight-hour solo journey in India pushed me to Christ. It was not until I got into the taxi for the return journey to Delhi that I realized that my fears had left me. It was the last day of Ramadan, so the streets were filled with Muslim men and children in celebration of the day. Groups of men surrounded our car as we drove through each small town. I had no cell phone and had forgotten to get contact phone numbers. I did not speak Hindi. My driver (who did not speak English) took a long detour off the two-lane paved road onto a dirt road that went for miles and miles past fields of sugarcane. (I only realized later that he was trying to avoid the Ramadan crowds.) Meanwhile, I suspected that my turbaned driver with his large gray mustache might die of a heart attack at any moment. He was ancient.

What an amazing eight hours! I wasn't sure I would make it to Delhi (Did Jesus have other plans for me?), but I was sure that he was in control of my situation. I had no doubt that God had heard my prayers. Timid as I am, I was never afraid because I knew he was with me. Jesus knows how desperately we will need him as we step into ministry, just as the first disciples did. Ministry often pushes us beyond our comfortable limits, just as Jesus pushed his disciples into situations that were beyond them. We are Christ's disciples for this age and he has not left us to figure things out on our own; he has sent his Spirit to lead us and remind us that he is with us, weaving every moment of our lives into the beautiful tapestry that is his kingdom coming. We can be confident that he is always with us and will always answer our prayers.

It does not take long to realize our need for Jesus as we experience the vulnerability that ministry introduces into our lives. When Josiah was a pastor, there were many times we would be having a conversation in public only to look up and see someone from the church listening to everything we said. It was not that we were talking about things that were interesting ("Would you like Grape Nuts or Frosted Flakes?") or confidential (although that has happened), but it was an unpleasant feeling to have our personal space unexpectedly invaded.

Ministry puts us on display. When we speak to people about the power of the gospel for redemption and deep change, they appropriately look to us to see the evidence of our words. That is why so many of us hide. We often see little evidence of the present power of the gospel in ourselves. We believe that ministry requires that we "put up or shut up," which is why we are so tempted to shade the truth about ourselves. Who would believe our words if they got a good look at our hearts? Every part of our lives is not simply on display, but on display in high definition with "enhanced picture quality." Every sin, weakness, struggle, and quirk is highlighted. Little wonder that we are tempted to hide, dodge, fake it, and correct people's impressions of us.

What we say and do every day is big and out there and (even if we are good at hiding) will eventually come to light. Jesus said it this way: "No one after lighting a lamp covers it with a jar or puts it under a bed, but puts it on a stand, so that those who enter may see the light. For nothing is hidden that will not be made manifest, nor is anything secret that will not be known and come to light" (Luke 8:16–17). If we want others to see the power of the gospel at work in a life, *we must be willing to be that life* put on display so that those around us will not only see God work, but also *how* he works. Then they will learn to step out in faith for themselves. Our willingness to live our lives displayed in high definition is not a negative side effect of ministry; rather it is the primary way God reveals himself through us. As people see how the gospel works to change us, they are encouraged to believe that it will also work to change them.

All believers are called to daily take up their cross and share Christ's good news with those around them. Every follower of Christ is called to minister in his kingdom. But those whom Christ has called to give up their lives for a ministry vocation face unique challenges and pressures. Like Jesus, we have a shepherd's heart and feel deeply for the sheep he has entrusted to our care. We carry their burdens. Because others look to us as examples of faith, Satan will continually come after us. We have potential to do great good as well as great harm for Christ's kingdom. And despite what Scripture teaches about the priesthood of every believer, those in ministry are consistently held to a higher standard. We have all heard stories of old clothes and used tea bags being sent to African missionaries, the assumption being that missionaries do not care about what they wear or a good cup of tea. Have you been judged by the model car you drive or where you grocery shop? Those of us who have devoted our lives to ministry have a special sisterhood of crazy stories, shared joys, and deep sorrows. (The things people say to us!)

Each chapter of this book starts with a topic of common interest to women in ministry—things that are challenging and difficult to talk about. Next, there are questions to help us sort through our thoughts and experiences and focus our prayers where we see the

Spirit working. Finally, each chapter ends with a Scripture meditation to reorient us to the promises of Christ *(Pause)* and the power of his Spirit at work *(Reset)* even in the hard places of our lives. We are in this fight together. No one is alone.

What Are Your Thoughts?

1. What does Christ's call to ministry look like for you in your present circumstance?

2. Where do you feel the press of ministry? What expectations from those you serve add to the pressure you feel? What pressures do you place on yourself?

3. What difficulties and struggles prevent you from connecting with God's love and care?

4. "If we want others to see the power of the gospel at work in a life, we must be willing to be that life, put on display so that those around us will not only see God work, but also how he works." How can this perspective change your approach to ministry?

Pause and Reset
Anticipation

But whatever gain I had, I counted as loss for the sake of Christ. Indeed, I count everything as loss because of the surpassing worth of knowing Christ Jesus my Lord. For his sake I have suffered the loss of all things and count them as rubbish, in order that I may gain Christ and be found in him, not having a righteousness of my own that comes from the law, but that which comes through faith in Christ, the righteousness from God that depends on faith—that I may know him and the power of his resurrection, and may share his sufferings, becoming like him in his death, that by any means possible I may attain the resurrection from the dead.

13

Not that I have already obtained this or am already
perfect, but I press on to make it my own, because Christ
Jesus has made me his own. [Sisters], I do not consider
that I have made it my own. But one thing I do: forgetting
what lies behind and straining forward to what lies ahead,
I press on toward the goal for the prize of the upward call
of God in Christ Jesus. Let those of us who are mature
think this way. (Philippians 3:7–15a)

We learn a lot about the nature of ministry when we read the
writings of Paul. As he writes to the Philippians from a jail cell,
Paul has followed Christ for many years. His description of where
ministry has taken him is revealing. He describes himself as having
lost everything to gain Christ. Ministry always brings suffering into
our lives. It always has a cost. When we think of Paul's humanity,
we get a sense of just how much of his life has been stripped away
as he sits in that jail cell. He has suffered the loss of all things and
we feel his loss.

Not only did he never marry, thus finding himself alone in that
way, now he is stuck in jail and cannot visit the spiritual children
into whom he has poured his life. Paul seems to have little in the
way of possessions. He relinquished his standing and future as a
brilliant Pharisee. He suffered many physical difficulties and dangers in his travels. From what we read in the New Testament, after
Paul's conversion, he picked up his cross and never looked back.
Giving all that we have is Christ's call to all believers, but that call
has many tangible results for those of us in vocational ministry.
We serve and lay down our lives so that others may come to know
Christ. As it did Paul, ministry ushers us into a lifestyle of suffering
and loss.

Suffering in ministry for the benefit of others has a particular
effect on us. It begins to pare down our excess. If you have bought
a new car lately or seen recent car advertisements, you know about

excess. These days the car we drive off the lot can have all of the comforts of home, act as our concierge, navigate our route, and offer a complicated menu of phone and music options activated by our voices—cool extras. In ministry we often fall into the temptation of leaning into our extras: all of the gifts, abilities, and experiences that God has given us.

Perhaps you are a wonderful teacher or an awesome cook. As we read in Philippians 3:4–6, when Paul refers to the confidence he could have had in his heritage, his accomplishments, and his abilities, we realize that Paul was also tempted in this way. But the uniqueness of the suffering that results as we bring the gospel to others is seen in its refining work. It strips away our dependence on the extras we tend to rely on. It pushes us to Christ. This is the effect of suffering on our ministry and it is a good one.

As we experience this suffering, instead of our lives overflowing with overpriced extras that highlight our progress, we start to look more like the pared down, rock-bottom-priced car that the salesman keeps hidden in the back. We find ourselves relying on Christ for even our most basic needs. That stripped down model is the Paul who is writing this letter from a jail cell.

Ministry brings suffering into our lives. It is the hardest gift for us to accept from God. None of us enjoys suffering and it is one aspect of ministry we are always trying to avoid. God brings his gift of suffering and our response is to begin negotiating for a different one. We want to return this gift for one we think would better meet our needs. This is why Paul's description of himself in Philippians 3 is so startling. We are attracted and repelled by it. We want his passion for Christ. We identify with his desire to know Christ and the power of his resurrection, but to share in the fellowship of Christ's sufferings is frightening. We struggle to believe that God would love us with the amazing-big-crazy-love we sing about, but at the same time bring suffering into our lives, especially ongoing suffering. Why does our heavenly Father seem at times to be steadily shoveling suffering into the lives of those he loves so deeply, when he could easily relieve it?

When our children struggled with reentry into American culture after life overseas as missionary kids, it was easy for me to be disappointed with God's performance. Until my children began to falter, I was oblivious to my expectations that God would provide a smooth path for them through the transitions of school and culture. After all, we had taken our family overseas for missionary work! All of us were often confused about the difficulties they faced and God's apparent silence in response to our desperate prayers. Our missionary choice brought deep suffering into our lives and the lives of our children.

Suffering is a tough beginning for a book about ministry, but like Paul, everyone I know who follows Christ into ministry suffers for their choice. Yet no one enjoys suffering. Our society works hard to avoid it and this fits well with our own desires. Even when we endure suffering, it is often for our own ends, like dieting to get into our skinny jeans. I have known people who have gone to remote mission fields to protect their children from the influences of American culture. Such decisions may cause suffering, but they are not how we share in the sufferings of Christ. We share in Christ's suffering as we suffer so that others may hear his gospel.

Because we are in ministry, our marriages, families, and personal lives are all affected by suffering. Great harm is done to our faith when this suffering surprises us. When God did not care for our children in the ways we anticipated, our faith was shaken. Great harm is done to our faith when suffering as a result of ministry is minimized or ignored—we kept making excuses for God rather than just admitting that we had no idea what he was doing. Rather than being derailed by suffering, Paul's faith was strengthened by it. An interesting aspect of Philippians 3, interwoven as it is with suffering, is that Paul does not present his suffering as an unfortunate result of ministry, but as a door to deeper identification with Christ.

Paul found that his suffering for the sake of the gospel brought him closer to Christ. If Paul's goal had been a worry-free life, he would have begrudged the suffering God's call brought him. But since Paul's goal was to know Christ, he experienced his suffering as a way to know many aspects of Christ that he would have otherwise missed. As we suffer the effects of laying down our lives for others, we need the comfort that only comes from Christ. We seek him out because he understands. We feel his mercy. When the burdens of others threaten to crush us, we hear the words of Christ, who comes alongside us to bear the weight of the yoke he has asked us to carry. We ponder this tender Christ.

We are forced by our suffering to wrestle with his teachings because we need to hear his voice to survive the confusion ministry brings. Only suffering makes us desperate enough to knock on the door of heaven until someone gives us an answer (Luke 11:5–13). We knock until our Father opens his door and welcomes us with his love and peace. Suffering keeps us from a life of glib answers and leads us into a life of listening to his Spirit. Jesus knew everything, but he was not a know-it-all. Suffering opens our eyes to the glory of our humble Savior. This is why Paul's letter to the Philippians overflows with joy—not at all what we would expect given Paul's circumstances! He knew this glorious Christ.

Paul is also confident and full of joy even as he suffers because he does not fear that his suffering is a result of God's inattention or displeasure. Suffering is a necessary cost of bringing the gospel to the nations. If we have placed our faith in Christ, we are safe in his righteousness and need never fear that our suffering is a result of his rejection or inattention. Rather, we can see our suffering as the cost of moving his kingdom forward and an open door into his presence.

As our kids struggled with reentry into the States and as we, still in Ireland, struggled with our helplessness to make life work for them, our combined suffering caused me to doubt God's goodness and love. Eventually I saw that I had been judging God to be unloving and unfaithful. As I began to confess as sin the audacious stance I had taken against him, I heard Christ's words of forgiveness and love and my heart began to soften. I saw that much of my devotion to God was contingent on his willingness to do things my way. Suffering became a door for me into the presence of Christ as he really is, not as I expected him to be.

We will never know what life would have been like for our family if we had not entered ministry, but we know we have all paid a price in suffering. The joy comes when we realize that our suffering is not random, but rather connects us to Christ. Then we can trust him to use our suffering to accomplish his ends. We may not understand how our suffering fits into his redemptive plan, but we can be honest about it. We can bring our suffering to Christ just as Paul did. Paul's suffering was real and extensive, but it did not define him, make him bitter, or cause him to doubt God's love or call on his life. Paul's suffering brought him into deeper fellowship with Jesus.

If our experience of Christ's love and gift of righteousness has little impact on our response to suffering, it may be time to take our spiritual pulse. How much of Christ have we come to know? Paul is not referring to knowledge *about* Christ in Philippians 3, but of a personal relationship *with* Christ. Has the gift of righteousness you have by faith in Christ given you firm ground on which to stand? Do you feel God's welcome as you approach his throne? Are you confident in his goodness and love even as you suffer? It is good to acknowledge the difficulties of ministry life, but they are not what give our lives meaning. If suffering has made us bitter, caused us to doubt Christ's love, or question his call on our lives, we need to look again at the ground we are standing on. Jesus did everything necessary to give us right standing with God. We are now God's children, part of his family with all the joys and benefits this brings. As we spend time with him, Christ will work a deeper assurance in our hearts that this is true—not just for others, but also for us. The benefits of his righteousness will work their way into our lives and give us the ability to endure suffering with joy, because our suffering connects us to Christ and all of his resources.

All of our needs are met and all of the promises of God are fulfilled in Christ, but we have to take hold of him by faith. We have to believe for *this* moment, even when it is difficult. We must join Paul in saying that yesterday's successes and failures are of no value to us (Philippians 3:7–8). This is where the rubber meets the road in regards to faith. Will I hold onto my hard-fought successes as the basis for my confidence? Or will I wallow in my failures and see myself as valueless to the kingdom?

There is no room in us for Christ if we are full of our successes. Likewise, there is no room in us for Christ if we are full of our failures. If we want to experience Christ's presence today, we must let go of all of our works, both good and bad. As believers, we have a moment-by-moment choice to decide whose work will define us. If we choose our own, we will find ourselves alone, filled with the pride of our successes or the despair of our failures. When we are able to rest in Christ's work for us (a righteousness from God that depends on faith), we will have space for Christ to dwell in every part of our lives.

Our experiences of the power of Christ's resurrection *and* the depth of fellowship we share in his sufferings are both necessary for ministry. Jesus moves his kingdom forward through us in both ways. When he displays his resurrection power through us as he answers our prayers, changes us visibly, and causes things to happen that are beyond what we could do, his kingdom moves forward. As we take up our crosses and give ourselves for others, thus sharing in his sufferings, Christ comes to us and we experience a deep fellowship with him. Through our suffering his kingdom also moves forward. The fellowship we have with Christ as he comforts us in suffering loosens our grip on this world, grounds our testimony in truth, and opens a conduit through which his Spirit can flow.

Paul was an amazing man, but even he was not up to the task he was given. How did he persevere through all the hardship and resistance he faced? How can we? The answer for Paul is the answer for us: *He no longer trusted in his ability to keep the law for his justification, rather he trusted in Christ to receive the gift of righteousness that he could not earn by his good works.* All the confidence he could have had in his brilliance, his knowledge of God's law, his religious pedigree and his Pharisaical zeal were put aside. Paul gave up everything to know Christ and to make him known. As we too begin to grasp that Jesus is our righteousness, we will be changed and given courage to step into ministry. Our source of strength is Christ's work for us.

It wasn't until I began to believe that God was no longer grading my performance—because Christ had been *graded* for me—that I began to realize the uniqueness of the gifts God had given me and how those gifts complemented Josiah's gifts. As long as I was trying to emulate the way God used Josiah and the women in ministry that I admired, I was a complete failure. When I began to appreciate that Christ had many ways of working and that my mix of gifts and abilities were useful tools in his hand, I was free to see how he had used me in the past. I could find great hope in his willingness to use me in the present and the future. Much of our struggle and unbelief come because we do not see the way God sees. Standing in the righteousness of Christ gives us God's perspective and strengthens us for all that comes our way.

We see from Paul's overflow of joy that he understood Christ's words when he encouraged his disciples to rejoice—not in a powerful ministry where demons were subject to them, but in the certainty that their names were written in heaven (Luke 10:20), thereby proving they belonged to him. We are not defined by ministry success or failure but by our inclusion into God's family. The strength, joy, and ability we need to persevere in ministry come, not from the ministry the Spirit produces through us, but from our belonging to God.

Jesus's purpose in calling us into ministry is to gather his people. His call gives definition and meaning to all of life. He does not call us into a job that is reasonable for us to manage or a job too big for us to handle. Rather, he puts us in a place where we will need him every day. Christ wants us to feel our need so that we will come to him. He knows that as our thoughts and emotions are full of him and as our faith is connected to him, his kingdom will move forward through us in ways we could never have imagined or done on our own. In his presence our focus turns away from ourselves toward the world he loves. We are filled with joy because we are his. We can awaken each morning knowing that he will meet us where we are and work through the smallest of faiths—a grain of mustard seed—to grow his kingdom into the largest of trees (Luke 13:19). Jesus invites us into the gathering of his people. Are *you* ready for some ministry?

Chapter 2
Proverbs 31 Remix

Remix: to rearrange or radically alter
a particular piece of music. (Wiktionary)

SOME OF MY favorite new music includes remixes of old standards. Much of it is innovative and creative, exposing a new generation of listeners to some wonderful old music. Remixing takes what is good in a song and reinterprets it to reach an audience that might otherwise miss it.

We can learn a lot from these innovative arrangers when it comes to the ministry stereotypes that affect many of us. Maybe it's time for us to remix those old standards to communicate Christ to a new generation that assumes we have little to say to them—and to an older generation of believers who have found church rules and traditions inadequate for their deep needs. If our desire is to free ourselves from the stereotypes and expectations people have of us, we have to begin by recognizing those stereotypes. People's expectations may push us into opportunities we would otherwise avoid so we don't want to toss them out altogether, but some of the roles we have inherited genuinely confuse the gospel message. They unwittingly give the impression that a response to the gospel means a life lived within a narrow band of cultural choices rather than a faith response to Christ. We need to examine our conventional roles to see their flaws and do a little remixing.

I often attend Christian ministry conferences and the outward differences among women always surprise me. Although some differences are a reflection of individuality, much of what I see reflects the stereotypes under which we labor. Our outward appearance often indicates the expectations others have of us. I have seen women with head coverings and long skirts while others look as if they've stepped out of a fashion magazine. Some dress casually; others wear heels. Some look trendy with piercings and tattoos and others wear styles that appear to be borrowed from their mothers. Our last pastorate was very casual, which fit me better than my time in Alabama, where in the 1980s women matched their purse with their shoes to go to the grocery store. Sometimes the stereotypes and expectations of our ministry cultures are not a bad fit, but at other times they can present a real challenge.

Expectations regarding our outward appearance is just one of many things we have to navigate in ministry. Many criticize how we spend our time and with whom we spend it. Some judge our standard of living. The pressure coming from those we serve is real, so sometimes it is easier to slide into the roles people have for us and do what they expect. But even if we conform to the outward expectations of others, we are still left with our own noisy consciences when we read about the virtuous woman of Proverbs 31, which many of us have been taught is God's standard for women. What does God think of our efforts to reflect the ideal portrayed in this passage? We may be able to dismiss or maneuver around the opinions people have about us, but what God thinks of us matters.

I began ministry life as the wife of a church planter in the American South. My cultural influences and ministry models were wrapped up in being the godly, virtuous woman I had been taught was represented in Proverbs 31. My models for ministry were extroverted, competent, self-confident women who seemed to navigate the church world effortlessly. I saw the woman of Proverbs 31 as a competent doer, and the ministry models I knew seemed like competent doers as well. My misunderstanding of this passage and my lack of access to the real lives of these women colluded to ensure my failure as a shy, introverted young woman who lacked confidence and a firm grasp of the gospel. My inexperience and inability to see the power these stereotypes had over me meant that I was defined by them—and by my failure to fulfill them—for many years.

I survived our first church plant because God kindly kept me so occupied that I had little time to examine my performance as a pastor's wife. We arrived in Louisiana fresh out of seminary with our children, ages one, three, and five. I loved being a mom and this role filled my days. We lived in the basement of the large house where our church met. In the fall of our first year, we started a school, which also met in the house. Our lives were full of people and things to do. (After two and a half years, the church built a building next door—whew!) I had a huge garden and learned to make jam, pickles, and anything else that fit in a jar. I sewed the children's clothes and made homemade gifts for Christmas. I learned to make gumbo, fry catfish, and host a crawfish boil. You get the idea. It was a rural community and life was busy.

Not only was life busy, we were also living in a tough area of rural Louisiana. Pretty much everything *had* happened in our town settled by Civil War deserters and criminals and anything *could* happen, which was often our experience. We saw God work in openly supernatural ways against much of the evil we experienced. We prayed for those who were demon-possessed, brushed up against organized crime, were persecuted by the community for pushing against the status quo, experienced the gospel's power to save those who seemed beyond saving, we saw God heal and answer all kinds of prayers. When the Holy Spirit began to move, life became very unpredictable. We never knew what the next phone call would bring. I think the women in the church pitied my "deer-in-the-headlights" response as I tried to navigate the craziness. Yet even with their gracious response and all of my busyness, my times of quiet reflection centered on my failure to meet the standards I thought God had for me.

After four years, we left Louisiana to plant a church in Alabama. Our new core group had been part of three failed church plants, but they were willing to give it one more try. Since this small group of families had experienced failure, their expectations for what the church should be had softened considerably. It was a great group. I love the dynamic of a church-planting situation better than any other in church work. It is all about creating something new. Working in an established church often feels like maintaining a well-oiled machine, but in church planting, you feel your need more practically and there is a constant air of expectation. What will God do? How will we pay the rent? Will anyone show up this Sunday? I like that.

As our young church began to grow, I began to resist pressure to get involved in children's ministries. Looking back, I am not sure what was going on with me. I did not want to sign up for the nursery. I did not want to teach Sunday school. I was unavailable for VBS. I would sing in the choir; and host dinners, Bible studies, and even the men's prayer breakfast week after week; but for some reason I did not want to work with children. The more pressure I felt, the harder I resisted. My zeal for church planting began to wane under the weight of all of the roles I felt obligated to fulfill.

I don't know how the women of the church viewed my excuses not to teach Sunday school or volunteer for the nursery. I no longer remember why I had decided to declare my independence that way. Of course, the place where the women gathered and got to know each other was in the context of these ministries, so I had isolated myself from many with whom I had some hope of friendship. Our home was not the center of church life as it had been in

Louisiana. Josiah left every morning for the office and came home at dinnertime, often just to eat and leave again for evening meetings. Church planting is hard, time-consuming work, since church planters usually have no staff and are happy for even a part-time secretary. Our weekends revolved around church. Friday afternoon and evening were set aside as our family time, but Saturdays were full of last-minute details for Sunday and Josiah's final preparations for morning and evening sermons, adult Sunday school, and the frequent Sunday night training session. Sunday itself was filled with church services, shared meals, and folks in between.

At this point I had not yet disconnected from ministry. I was just trying to break out of what I saw as the stereotypical role of a pastor's wife in the late 1980s. I attempted to teach Bible studies but was not very good at it. I think I knew God was calling me into more than just church activities, but I could not figure out what that would look like. It seemed that whatever I tried to do, my conscience would shout, "Not good enough, you should have done more." As the years went by, I began to disconnect from ministry altogether. I struggled with depression. I had great kids and a husband who loved me, but I could not escape my failure to be what I thought I should be. I frequently asked God why he would call me into a life where he knew I would fail. I decided that God must not like me very much.

For women in ministry, it is easy to get tangled in Proverbs 31. We have been told that this woman should be the pattern for our lives. We are taught that women in ministry, whether single or married, are to be shining examples of virtue that other women can follow. Single women often feel at a disadvantage when the banner of Proverbs 31 is raised because the woman's life described in the passage is organized around her family and household. Is true virtue unattainable for women who are single? Staff women in churches are often at a loss when they seek to apply its principles to their actual job responsibilities. Does the passage only speak to the home life of married women? Regardless of our jobs and marital status, we all have to do some creative interpretation to make the passage fit our lives. Yet even in our confusion about Proverbs 31, we are still seduced by the idea that we can become the amazing superwoman described. Whether married or single, we are led to believe that we can become the women God wants us to be by working hard to follow the principles and examples laid out in this passage. Only when God puts us in a desperate place where those principles and examples become hollow and ineffectual are we open to our need for Christ—not as our helper, but as our remedy for present sin and need, even as believers and women in ministry.

In 1991 I was in that place. After thirteen years of trying and failing to be what I thought a pastor's wife should be, I knew I could not live up to the examples I had been given. Josiah had long given up trying to help me. I felt utterly alone. Even as I write these words I remember the deep pain of my failure and what it felt like to realize the foolishness of it. I was ready to hear what God had to say to me. I began to see the deep pride that had kept me from simply going to Jesus, feeling that I was somehow beyond his help. I began to see how my cries for help were more like a fist in God's face, demanding that he help me attain my goals, rather than a humble heart's request. I saw that much of my failure and guilt was driven by my desire for a good reputation and my need to receive some credit for my good works. As you may have noticed, the story was centered on *me*: my successes and my failures. By unconsciously making the standard of my life the mythic ministry model I saw in Proverbs 31, I had become the center. No wonder I felt miserable and alone.

The list of my sins is not important. Our experiences and lists will vary. The point is that I started to see that my sin was much broader and deeper than I had imagined and that God had provided a remedy for my sin. In the 1990 movie *The Freshman,* we are drawn into the story of a young man who though trying hard to do the right thing, cannot stop getting himself deeper and deeper into trouble. Toward the end of the movie he stands on a pier reflecting on the freedom of being completely *screwed*. He is utterly powerless to alter his situation. That is a perfect image of the moment when we see the enormity of our sin—when our sin is so huge and unmanageable that we have no hope of dealing with it. We are powerless to fix it. In that moment the cross becomes real to us; the cross makes sense. As long as sin is manageable and reasonable, we are stuck carrying it around, but when it can only be dealt with from outside of us, we can be free of it.

As long as we are in ministry, there will be stereotypes and roles that people expect us to fulfill. When we are confident of God's welcome because of Christ's work for us, we can be free from the power that people's opinions have over us. We will have to engage their expectations at times, but that is different from living under their weight. We may not always have the approval of the people around us, but we have God's approval because of the righteousness of his Son. As we are strengthened by these gospel realities, we will find ourselves better able to serve without the extra baggage of roles and stereotypes.

What Are Your Thoughts?

1. Often the particular ways our group measures spirituality are invisible to us. For example, some may criticize those who use drums in their worship; others may criticize those who wear a suit and tie. The idea that "our group is more spiritual because of the way we do things" has a deep impact on our ability to communicate with those from other Christian subcultures and especially non-Christians. How does your group measure spirituality? How do these rules of spirituality negatively affect you? How do they impact your ability to communicate the gospel to people outside your group?

2. Read Proverbs 31. List some of the traits described that have created guilt or pride in your life.

3. Review the stereotypes that affected me. Use my list as a springboard to make a list of the stereotypes that push you around.

4. Ask God to show you sins you have been managing instead of taking to Christ for forgiveness.

Pause and Reset
We Are Deeply Loved

The words of King Lemuel. An oracle that his mother taught him:

An excellent wife who can find? She is far more precious
   than jewels.
The heart of her husband trusts in her, and he will have
   no lack of gain.
She does him good, and not harm, all the days of her life.
She seeks wool and flax, and works with willing hands.
She is like the ships of the merchant; she brings her food
   from afar.
She rises while it is yet night and provides food for her
   household and portions for her maidens.
She considers a field and buys it; with the fruit of her
   hands she plants a vineyard.
She dresses herself with strength and makes her arms
   strong.
She perceives that her merchandise is profitable. Her
   lamp does not go out at night.
She puts her hands to the distaff, and her hands hold the
   spindle.
She opens her hand to the poor and reaches out her
   hands to the needy.
She is not afraid of snow for her household, for all her
   household are clothed in scarlet.

She makes bed coverings for herself; her clothing is fine
linen and purple.
Her husband is known in the gates when he sits among
the elders of the land.
She makes linen garments and sells them; she delivers
sashes to the merchant.
Strength and dignity are her clothing, and she laughs at
the time to come.
She opens her mouth with wisdom, and the teaching of
kindness is on her tongue.
She looks well to the ways of her household and does not
eat the bread of idleness.
Her children rise up and call her blessed; her husband
also, and he praises her:
"Many women have done excellently, but you surpass
them all."
Charm is deceitful, and beauty is vain, but a woman who
fears the LORD is to be praised.
Give her of the fruit of her hands, and let her works praise
her in the gates. (Proverbs 31:1, 10–31)

Note: A key to understanding the passage is to look at the meaning of the Hebrew word that the ESV translates as excellent. The KJV translates the same word as virtuous. There are many meanings for this Hebrew word depending on its context. A reliable source[1] offers this definition of the Hebrew word in the Proverbs 31 context: ability, efficiency, often involving moral worth. The aspect of moral worth adds an element of meaning that can be lost by the word excellent. The woman of Proverbs 31 is praised from the inside out. Her inner beauty is revealed through her excellent deeds. Virtuous is a helpful translation.

To clear up our confusion and understand God's opinion of us, it is time to take a fresh look at Proverbs 31 and do a little remixing.

Hearing the particulars of this passage has been a defining moment in the life of many female believers. Some of us were in a women's Bible study when the slow light of impossibility dawned and we thought, "Is this for real?" The passage begins with a rhetorical question to which the obvious answer is that "virtuous women" are scarcer than hen's teeth. In the words of Elizabeth Bennett to Mr. Darcy, "I am no longer surprised at your knowing 'only' six accomplished women. I rather wonder now at your knowing 'any.'"[2] The standard is beyond our reach. The simple question, "Where are the virtuous women?" that begins the passage completely infects our view of Christian womanhood. It is our nemesis, meeting us around every corner. Its pursuit is unrelenting, and our response is either to take up the challenge or run for the hills. It is rare to meet a woman who views this passage without some measure of pride or guilt.

If virtuous women are so rare, how are we to approach the passage? Is it up to us to work hard to make ourselves one of the virtuous few? Are we condemned if we just admit defeat and set it aside? Would it be helpful to approach the passage verse by verse and give it a current cultural interpretation? Let's try it and read it through the context of our lives in today's world.

How might that look for us? Perhaps shopping online for the exotic ingredients required for our gourmet cooking would qualify as bringing our food from afar: very trendy. If we had an Etsy account, we could sell our handmade goods all over the world. That seems impressive. We might keep strong by doing yoga or working out at the local gym. Is the virtuous woman limber and buff? Since she plans for the future, why not get an iPad with an E*trade app? To tackle this Proverbs 31 list, we will need to be adept at multi-tasking, with closets organized and leftovers labeled.

Apparently, TV, movies, and Angry Birds are idle pursuits for the ever-productive woman of virtue. Still, we might justify social media and texting as useful ministry tools. In the 1970s this passage was used to teach me that I should get up at 5 a.m. to read the Bible because the virtuous woman gets up while it is still dark—never mind that she was rising early to see that her household and servants are fed. This woman is no slacker. To accomplish all that she does, our lives would have to be well-oiled machines with no real people to slow us down.

Even so, that is just the *doing*. In verse 28 things get downright personal. Who of us wants to be evaluated by whether or not our children rise up and call us blessed? Many older women tell stories of children who expect to be supported into adulthood, blame parents for their difficulties, and are critical of what they see as their parents' failure to raise them in a nurturing environment. Life has not turned out the way our Christian parenting books promised us it would—not even close. The world is a difficult place to navigate and many of our children have struggled to make their way.

For all that, younger women are under great pressure to produce a generation of children that are not weighed down by rules and laws. A perfect atmosphere of grace in the home is the high standard many young women have set for themselves. Yet regardless of how much we desire our families to be centered on the graciousness of Christ, our sin intrudes and corrupts our best intentions. Each generation works to correct the failures of the previous one, but we live in a fallen world and no matter how hard we try, how many books we read, and how much progress we make, we still fail to be the perfect parents our children need. We have yet to produce a generation of unfettered children. Many times our children do return to bless us, but sometimes they do not.

Using Proverbs 31 as our checklist for spiritual maturity will not create faith or obedience in us. It can only produce pride or discouragement. Reading it this way never gets us beyond ourselves into the presence of Christ. I have known women who have listed the virtuous woman's traits and measure their day by how many virtues they are able to emulate. Of course, this leads to some imaginative interpretations, but if we are creative enough, we can use the passage to feel good about our success and productivity. Whether we take the descriptions of her virtue literally and make linen garments to sell (v. 24) or reinterpret each facet of her life with a modern counterpart, how does that help us? When will we know we have done enough? Regardless of our strategies in approaching this passage, we will never manage and organize this superlist into submission.

As we think about this passage, it might be helpful to note that the woman described in Proverbs 31 will have great wealth and influence because her husband is the king. Much of her life is filled with buying and selling, dealing with merchants, and organizing servants. Unless we have both wealth and power available to us, we cannot model our lives after her. We can only extrapolate principles from the traits that are mentioned. The result of focusing on the principle behind each trait and comparing ourselves with it is that we are constantly evaluating our performance. How am I reflecting the qualities of Proverbs 31 today? Did I succeed today, perhaps by knitting a sweater or working out at the gym? Or did I fail today because I never made it to the grocery store and served peanut butter sandwiches for supper? Whether we succeed or fail, the focus remains on *us*.

Although the whole book is about reaping and sowing, comparing the wise person who fears the Lord with the fool who lives as if there is no God, Proverbs 31 takes reaping and sowing to a whole new level. This woman buys a field and plants it. We feel certain that before you know it, she will be pouring wine for dinner. There is no mention of bugs, disease, too much rain, too little rain, or an early frost. Anyone who has ever tried to grow something knows that it is always fraught with challenge. I had a hard time growing tomatoes even in the rich, black soil of Louisiana! Bugs, wilt, and blight were my enemies. Yet at the end of Proverbs 31, the fruits of her labor commend her. She is praised for her success. She seems almost godlike, as if whatever she imagines, she can do.

We are encouraged to read the passage as supplemental commandments for Christian womanhood. We are tempted to read it this way because we don't know what else to do with it. We wrongly read it as a reminder that God has an ideal woman in mind and we had best get after it! The concept of the ideal woman is deeply ingrained in us as daughters and as mothers, and in this passage we see King Lemuel's mother's (Proverbs 31:1) deep desire for him to find the perfect wife—every mother's desire for her son. He is simply recounting her advice to him. It is when I read her advice to her son as God's advice to me that things get weird.

If the passage is not a description of the principles of godly womanhood, what could it mean? Is it pointing us in a different direction? From our post-resurrection of Christ's vantage point, we can see that the intent of the passage is broader than the quagmire of details that bog us down. At first reading we hear King Lemuel's mother giving him advice for finding the perfect wife. Lemuel responds by writing a love poem, most likely doing a little hopeful dreaming as he does so. It is an acrostic poem using successive letters of the Hebrew alphabet, so we cannot help but wonder what traits would have been added or subtracted had the Hebrew alphabet had a different number of letters. King Lemuel lays out all the qualities he longs to find in the perfect woman who will become his bride and queen. Are these the traits of Christian womanhood to which we should aspire?

As Lemuel begins his poetic description, the assumption is that her position as his wife and his wealth at her disposal will enable her to accomplish the amazing things he describes. This is an important point that colors the entire passage. Lemuel is a powerful, wealthy king who is looking for a woman who will use his vast resources for great good, a woman he can trust. He wants to lavish her with his love and wealth, and he anticipates that she will respond to that love in amazing ways. He wants a woman who will give herself to him completely when he chooses her as his bride and queen. His expectations are high as he describes the way she will devote herself to his good and the good of his household. She holds nothing back as she opens her hands to the poor, sharing the king's wealth with them. She is creative in her loving and generous in her giving. She does not shrink back from the trust he has placed in her. What a woman! King Lemuel has high hopes for the woman he will choose.

As we seek to understand Proverbs 31, we read it differently than did those in Old Testament times who were looking forward to the Messiah. We now read it through the lens of the life, death, and resurrection of Christ. Many things are clear to us that Old Testament believers did not understand. Since the coming of Christ changed how we read the Old Testament, it would be good to see how his coming changes our understanding and application of this passage.

We might begin by viewing King Lemuel as a "type" or forerunner of Christ. With Christ at the center of the passage, we see it from a different vantage point and its meaning is clearer. There is a perfect bride reflected in these verses, although I am not certain that King Lemuel ever found her. This vision of the perfect bride is Christ's view of us, his church. He is the wealthy King-Bridegroom; we are his bride. Through our understanding of the New Testament, we can begin to see the beauty and depth of this passage and understand that, oddly enough, it applies to both women and men, single or married. How appropriate that a book on wisdom would end with the secret wisdom of God whose future King-Bridegroom would change everything.

With Christ as our focus, we can appreciate the amazing truths this passage reveals. Our King's bountiful provision for us, his bride, gives us all we need to be extravagantly creative as we love and serve him and seek to bless those around us. We may view the elements of our day as tasks to be completed and relational obligations to fulfill, but this is not God's desire for us. He calls us into a life of creativity and joy as we wake each morning. He wants us to serve our king with a passion and imagination that requires our full engagement. Proverbs 31 encourages us to move beyond our lists to something more extravagant. The father of the bride in the 2002 movie *My Big Fat Greek Wedding* describes many of us well in his disparaging description of his daughter's future in-laws as *dry toast*. Getting through the day and checking things off our lists, even a Proverbs 31 list, is dry toast living. Our king has more for us.

Proverbs 31 highlights the wealth available to the bride of the King. We often view ourselves as poor and without resources, but the teaching of the New Testament is clear: Jesus became poor so that we might become rich. It is our unbelief that keeps us in the poorhouse. It is from the wealth of the king and her position as his wife that the virtuous woman is able to be and do all the things represented in this passage. Out of that relationship she prospers, and from *his* resources she is blessed and able to bless others.

We also see a beautiful picture of a husband completely delighted and proud of his wife. The passage reveals a remarkable truth—the heart of this husband trusts his wife. What an amazing way to think of Christ, our Bridegroom. He is so confident in his choice of us as his bride that he has no problem placing his complete trust in us. If we read the passage from Christ's perspective, how it changes our response! In the safety and joy of this extravagant relationship, our wifely hearts are free to overflow with all sorts of creative responses; we are no longer limited by the list in Proverbs 31. Because our King-Bridegroom delights in us, we can use his resources with freedom and creativity to serve and bless those around us.

As we mature in our relationship with Christ, we come to realize that reading Scripture as a "how-to-live-the-Christian-life" manual does not help us find him in its pages. How cruel that women have been encouraged to see the "virtuous woman" as a law of Christian womanhood rather than a lavish relationship in which to rejoice!

Because of what Jesus did for us on the cross, God is not judging and grading our implementation of the Proverbs 31 ideal. We are freed from its condemnation. Jesus has been judged. Jesus has performed perfectly. A passage that was once a heavy burden now becomes a source of joy. We have been called to something better and deeper. Jesus has called us into relationship as his bride. We belong to him. The power of ministry stereotypes and role models crumbles in his presence and we can leave them behind.

Christ's unlimited resources are available for our use as we step into ministry each day. How do we spend the wealth our King-Bridegroom has placed at our disposal? Are we dry toast women that only do what is required of us? Or are our lives filled with a passionate desire to create new ways to love God and those around us? Those we mentor will pattern themselves after us. Even those who look to us as casual examples can see the difference between passion and duty.

Reading Proverbs 31 in light of what Jesus has done for us encourages us to see ourselves through his eyes. Christ deeply loves and rejoices over his bride. Our faith and ability to trust him and step into ministry grow stronger as we understand that we are the ones he has chosen. When we read Proverbs 31 as Christ's love letter to *us*, his true opinion of *us*, we begin to understand how deeply we are loved. The riches of his love and grace ignite a passion in us that responds to him without hesitation or reservation. We may look foolish at times, but we hold nothing back as we love and serve the King who has made us his bride.

Chapter 3

The Gospel Revisited

Revisit: to visit again; to reconsider
or re-experience something. (Wiktionary)

THE DISCIPLES MISUNDERSTOOD much of what Jesus taught about himself and his kingdom before he was glorified (e.g., John 12:16 and John 16:12–14). God's redemption plan was not clear until the coming of his Spirit as evidenced by Peter's sermon in Acts 2. We hear the disciples' confusion in the last question they ask Jesus: "Lord, will you at this time restore the kingdom to Israel?" (Acts 1:6). They had witnessed his crucifixion. They had been with him after his resurrection and still this is their last question. They may seem thick-headed to us, but here before them was a man who could heal the sick, defeat demons, feed thousands with a few morsels of food, raise the dead, and even come back to life after being murdered. It appeared to be the perfect time for this powerful Messiah to restore the kingdom to Israel. Every Old Testament believer longed for the "Son of Man" described in Daniel 7:13–14 to descend from heaven, destroy their enemies, and establish his kingdom. It was not odd that the disciples would expect Jesus the Messiah to establish a physical kingdom on earth.

Jesus openly referred to himself as the Son of Man when he stood before the chief priests and Jewish council (Mark 14:62). Everyone knew what he meant when he gave himself that title, which is why the Sanhedrin was in uproar. This specific, powerful prophetic title that Christ applied to himself also had a deep impact on the disciples. It is why they still expect that earthly kingdom even in their last conversation with Jesus. The mystery of God's salvation plan had not yet been revealed. That would begin at Pentecost (Acts 2:1–4).

I have great sympathy for the disciples in their difficult and confusing last moments with Christ. They had been through the trauma of the crucifixion and the euphoria of the resurrection. They had given up everything to be part of Christ's coming kingdom. As we read the Gospels, it is easy to imagine them waking every day wondering, "Is this the day that Jesus will free Israel from her oppressors?" His answer to this question on his final day with them seems less than satisfactory. "He said to them, 'It is not for you to know times or seasons that the Father has fixed by his own authority'" (Acts 1:7). Instead, he left them with the promise of his Spirit and a mission to take his message to the ends of the earth (Acts 1:8).

Christ's answer to his disciples must have been disappointing, but I think he offered it with tenderness and compassion. Although he had previously called them "slow of heart to believe" (Luke 24:25), he does not do so here. He was about to leave them and he knew their hearts were breaking. He loved these men. When we do not feel as if Jesus is listening to us or giving us the answers we seek, this exchange with his disciples reminds us that God's plans may unfold in unusual ways that make little sense to us in the moment. But he is always working, even when we cannot see it or understand what he is doing. Today God is still working in the world in surprising, unexpected ways.

Why talk about the disciples' struggles to believe in a chapter about the gospel? Their struggles are revealing because we have much in common with them. Our expectations cloud our vision. Even after the coming of the Spirit, we still look for physical deliverance more often than we might think. The "spiritual stuff" like forgiveness of sin and the fruits of the Spirit are great, but often what we really want is a growing church full of people who appreciate us, a functional missionary team that does not stress us out, true friends who actually pursue us, happy marriages, thoughtful roommates, acknowledgment for our contribution to the work, a healthy bank balance, a car that starts each morning, and a vacation that is not in a borrowed place we have to clean before we leave. Sometimes our expectations combine with ministry pressures to make it hard to see that the abundant life Christ offers is simply found in the gospel. Our lists are much longer. Just as the disciples filled Christ's words with their own meanings and missed what was happening right in front of them, our prejudices and expectations influence our prayers and Scripture study so that we can miss the powerful gospel at work all around us as we, too, fill Christ's words with our own meanings and expectations.

Let's look more closely at this gospel we so easily confuse and take for granted. What could it say to us that we haven't already heard? Wouldn't it be great if the things we need for life and ministry were available to us through the gospel, something that we already know? What is this gospel that is so familiar to us?

The gospel, simply stated, is this: Jesus paid the penalty for our sin by his death on the cross and then conquered death by his resurrection to bring eternal life to all who believe. His Spirit changes our hearts to love God and want to please him. Our faith in his work on our behalf is credited to us as righteousness, so that as we stand before a Holy God, not only is all of our sin forgiven, but also we are declared righteous before him. Because of Jesus, God adopts us into his family with all the benefits that come from being his children. He no longer deals with us in judgment and wrath because he has poured all that judgment and wrath onto Christ. Instead, God welcomes us as his beloved children. As his children, we become a part of his plan to redeem the nations. His children are also his ambassadors to the world. Yet the certainty of our relationship with God is not in our ability to be obedient children or effective ambassadors, but only in the finished work of Christ for us. The true guarantee that we belong to God is the presence of his Spirit within us (2 Corinthians 1:22). Jesus has done everything necessary to bring us into a right relationship with the holy, triune God. Yet, even as I summarize this message, I don't think I have said anything you don't already know. So, let's look at each part of the gospel message to see what it says to us today.

First, Jesus paid the penalty for our sin by his death on the cross.

When we understand how much God hates sin, the guilt of our offenses is difficult to carry. If we are willing to confess our sin to him, he will forgive our sin and remove its burden of guilt. The good news that Christ forgives sinners is our good news. When God removes the weight of our sin, we are more than relieved; we are transformed. With the penalty of our sin lifted, we become new people who can make new choices. Our reconciliation to God opens vistas of possibilities to us.

When Josiah and I began raising financial support to go to Ireland as missionaries in 1992, the transforming power of the gospel was what enabled me to stand in front of a group and talk about Christ. I am not a natural public speaker, though I am married to someone who is. When I stand in front of a group, my thoughts get muddled. When Josiah stands before a group, he comes alive. Over the years my public speaking skills have improved, but it will never be something that makes me feel completely comfortable or competent. The freedom I have found to speak before a group is one fruit of the gospel working change in me. The gospel helps me to understand that Christ does not expect me to turn in a perfect performance or be someone I am not. He wants me to step out in faith and believe that he will use me. The fruit of Christ's gift of forgiveness is that we no longer have to prove ourselves worthy of it. The freedom we find as our experience of his favor grows turns our attention away from ourselves to Christ who leads us to love and serve others, often beyond our gifts and comfortable limitations.

Being assured of our forgiveness in Christ also gives us courage to admit our sin when the Spirit convicts us or others point it out. If we deny it or "rename" our sin as something we can manage, we will once again be stuck carrying it around with us. When we refer to our gossip as concern, our criticism as honesty, or our anger as frustration, we no longer need forgiveness for sins. We have no sin to be forgiven! We begin to regain our weight of sin. But if we take our sin to Christ and ask for his cleansing and forgiveness, we can leave the burden with him. Although this is a simple enough process, it is hard to do. Each trip we make to the cross is a blow to our pride, an admission of our failure. It is evidence that despite all God has done for us, we still struggle to obey him and persist in choosing other things to satisfy our needs and desires. It is humbling.

More recently, as Josiah and I have worked to fix up the house we purchased outside Philadelphia, some old relational patterns from our early years of marriage have resurfaced. Both of us have been surprised at the intensity of these patterns. (My complaint: "You are not helping!" His complaint: "You are too critical!") This is spiritual warfare. Do I give in to the deep discouragement I feel when it seems that I will never change? Or do I run to Christ with my sin and once again receive his forgiveness?

I am a comparatively old believer who has been in ministry many years, but I still have a choice each day. If I will take my sin to Jesus, he will relieve me of its burden. But when I see the entangling grip sin has on me, I must admit that taking my sin to him is hard at times. He's heard it so many times before. We must push through our doubts that taking our sin to him will make any difference at all. Accepting Christ's forgiveness and his gift of righteousness is always an act of faith. If I am willing to stop feeling defensive or sorry for myself, and turn to him in the hard places of my life, he will meet me. He follows his bad news of "You are critical" with the comfort of true forgiveness, the amazing gift of righteousness, and tender reminders of his promise to complete the work he has begun in me (Philippians 1:6). He meets me, and in his presence I find comfort, relief, and joy. It puts my sin in its proper place: under his blood.

Ministry also puts us in harm's way. Satan comes after us. He wants us to be weak and ineffective. The battle for faith is often as simple as believing that Jesus will receive me with joy, change me, and use me in his kingdom work, even when I am caught in the same old sin. At other times the battle for faith is to believe that I need his help at all. Both responses keep me from actually going to Christ.

The bad news that I am critical and hard on those around me is a sign that I have lost the sense of my own sinfulness and the grace God daily shows me. In other words, I may know the facts of the gospel, but have forgotten that I need it too. In times of stress I often forget my need for Jesus and revert to old patterns of behavior. This is often the source of many of my conflicts with Josiah. I am blind to my own sin and keenly aware of his. One friend of mine responds to stress by doing everything for herself. She becomes incapable of letting others lend a hand. Another friend responds by being so critical of herself that she finds herself apologizing for every little thing. When we lose sight of the grace that continually covers our sin, we won't have a gracious response to those whose sin impacts us, nor will we be able to be encouraged by them. When we forget our need for God's grace, we have little patience with those who don't measure up to our standards or for their disruptive words.

Our present understanding and experience of how far short we fall of God's perfect standard (even as believers) will make us more tenderhearted regarding the struggles of others. The remedy for our sin is the remedy for theirs. People respond to what comes from our hearts rather than our mouths. Usually we experience this when our good words are ignored because people are responding to the judgment they feel from us rather than our insightful comments. But when we are experiencing our need for Christ's cleansing blood, our words of encouragement to others will ring true and bring hope. Working for the good of those around us without pushing our agenda into their lives or seeking to change them for our convenience is a result of experiencing Christ's grace for our sin today.

When the gospel is at work in us, we experience life differently. It isn't that we are *trying* to experience life differently, we just do. I have been amazed at the ways God has softened and changed me over the years, even while I struggle with remaining sin. In our last pastorate in Asheville, I worked tirelessly to fix up our three-bedroom rancher. I loved that house! It was perfect for us since our children were grown and gone. We had rented houses all during our missionary years, so this was the first house I had been able to make my own since the children were young. I enjoyed scouring thrift stores for the mid-century furniture we love, choosing paint colors, and putting it all together.

When we decided to leave the church and rejoin Serge, the number one question I was asked was about that house: How could I possibly leave it? Everyone who knew me had seen its transformation. The funny thing was that it wasn't hard to leave that house at all. Even I found my response surprising. The house sold after a few months; we packed our belongings and never looked back. That was a totally unexpected fruit of the gospel. Leaving my favorite house was not a sacrifice but a door to the next adventure. For a homebody like me, that was no small miracle. I left excited, without regret.

For fifteen months of raising support, we slept in spare rooms, borrowed apartments, and motels, but I never regretted the decision to pull up stakes and start anew at age fifty-five. My unexpected positive response to the loss of that house and our temporary homelessness was not because I am a super spiritual person. Ask Josiah; I still have a long way to go. There were many days that I was grumpy from my lack of personal space. But experiencing Jesus's welcoming forgiveness over the years has changed me. I am more willing to take my everyday sin to Jesus, which has changed my values and worked gratitude in me. I love the moment when I know Christ is speaking to me. I am so thankful that he continues to lead us into new ministry. Leaving our cozy home in Asheville, North Carolina may have been a sacrifice, but it was so clear that Jesus was moving us into something new that I hardly noticed. It was hard to leave our friends and our church, but not our home. As we slog through the everyday, it is hard to believe that taking our sin to Christ and experiencing his forgiveness will transform us, but take heart. It truly does change us.

Second, God counts us as righteous when we put our trust in Jesus.

Not only did Jesus's death take away our sin, it also gives us Christ's righteousness as our own. We can see the gospel at work in us as we embrace this gift. Our confidence in the gift is evidenced in our approach to God.

Have you ever noticed the perfect posture that typifies members of the military or a ballet company? Their years of pursuing these distinctive callings have made their posture elegant and natural. Confidence in Christ's righteousness for us gives us perfect posture spiritually as we stand before God's throne. After years of standing in that righteousness, it becomes more natural for us to approach God, not with arrogance, but with boldness. That's because our standing depends on his good works, not our own. As we stand in his righteousness, we know we will be received with joy. As we grow confident in our Father's welcome, we won't hesitate to ask him for the mercy and grace we need (Hebrews 4:16)—even when our struggles result from our own sins. We no longer stand before God ashamed or defeated because he has declared us righteous.

During a renewal conference in Eastern Europe, I was assigned to mentor a single woman who was serving in an extremely difficult place. It was a physically challenging place to live, culturally male-dominated, and with an organization that put great pressure on their workers for statistical results. Many people remarked to me during the conference about this woman's success in ministry. She was upbeat and slightly amused that she would need mentoring in basic Christian ideas, especially the gospel.

When we got around to talking about sin patterns or sins that she might be struggling with, she did not have an answer. She could not think of one sin to talk about. Her understanding of the righteous standing she had before God because of Christ was so tenuous, and the pressure she felt for a perfect performance so great, that after a week of meeting each day, I was unsure if she had allowed herself one honest moment with me. At the end of our time she gave me a lovely gift (which resulted in many remarks regarding her deep kindness). It broke my heart to leave this dear sister working so hard to please God and those around her in such a desolate place without the assurance of God's good opinion of her. I left, praying that the Spirit would interrupt the fear and pride that kept her from believing that Jesus had done enough to make her righteous and welcomed in God's presence. Almost everybody I know in ministry works hard, but hard work is never enough to win God's favor. Only Christ's works are truly righteous and pleasing to God.

Trusting in Christ's righteousness for our relationship with God will deeply affect our approach to ministry. This may be a new idea for some of us. While at a luncheon with campus ministry workers (both women in primary ministry and wives of those in ministry) the conversation turned to Christ's work for us. It became quite lively as many had a question or a story or a what-about? These women had been so used to their relationship with Christ being organized around what they did for God that they were completely captivated by the idea that their relationship with God rested on what he had done for them. They realized that students would be much more responsive to someone with a grateful heart, who knew God's love and present need for a Savior, than someone who focused on the disciplines of Christian living.

When I was a student, the women who had a deep influence on me were not those who kept up with how many quiet times I had each week, but several women who were open and real about themselves and whose conversations were filled with Christ. One in particular would always say the same thing to me: "Barbara, you need to love Jesus and hate sin." My quiet times have waxed and waned over the years, but after almost forty years I still remember her love for Jesus and her advice. Christ is the center of our lives.

When our standing before God rests on anything other than the finished work of Christ, we will never be certain of his response to us no matter how much time we spend reading our Bibles or doing good works. One simple way to see whose work we are trusting today is to think about our prayers. If we are uncertain of God's welcome when we come with our requests, we will judge his acceptance and love by whether or not he answers our prayers with a yes. If we aren't sure of God's acceptance and love, we will have trouble when he doesn't respond as we think he should. Often our frustration results in prayerlessness. Why bother to pray if God isn't going to give us what we want? When we are praying without confidence in his welcome, we struggle to believe that God will take our prayers seriously. We make excuses for him. We don't pray in faith, believing that he hears and answers us. We don't pray much at all. Our uncertainty of his welcome affects every aspect of our relationship with him, but it is seen clearly in what we pray and how often we pray.

When we are confident of his gift of righteousness, we *will* pray. We will be changed and the world will be changed as we pray with eyes of faith. James 5:16b says it this way: "The prayer of a righteous person has great power as it is working." The righteousness James refers to is not our works of righteousness, which Isaiah compares to a polluted garment (Isaiah 64:6), but the perfect work of Christ, which Paul refers to as "the righteousness of God through faith in Jesus Christ for all who believe" (Romans 3:22). The content and frequency of our prayers help us to see whose righteousness we are trusting. If we are standing in Christ's righteousness, our prayers will be bold and our expectation of God's loving response will be sure. We will continue to trust him even when his answers make no sense to us. As Christ's righteousness impacts our lives, we realize that James 5:16b describes us: *we* are that righteous person, and it is our prayers that have great power as they are working.

Third, because of the work of Christ for us, God makes us his children.

Our sins have been forgiven; we have been given the gift of righteousness. What more could God do for us? Amazingly, he has brought us into his family. If having our sins forgiven feels passé and righteousness is a vague concept to connect with, God has one more arrow in his quiver to pierce our tough exterior. He has made us his children with all the benefits this entails (Galatians 3:29; Romans 8:16–17). He chose us and adopted us into his family. When we enter his presence, we find ourselves running to him and shouting, *Abba,* Father! This is a heartfelt greeting that only a well-loved child expresses (Galatians 4:4–7). Our Father has made us co-heirs with Christ, his firstborn. All that belongs to Christ now belongs to us. As our Father, God is often able to penetrate our defenses and speak to our embattled hearts. Don't be discouraged if this is not yet your daily experience. Take yourself to God and ask him for what you need today. "He who did not spare his own Son but gave him up for us all, how will he not also with him graciously give us all things?" (Romans 8:32). This is the gracious, generous Father to whom we appeal.

Living our lives out of these gospel truths does not come naturally to us. More often than not, we deny our sin or make excuses as if *we* would never actually sin on purpose. We want people to think well of us and, although we rarely admit it, we find our need for Jesus's righteousness offensive at times. A part of us wants Christ to be the center of things, but we like being the center of things more often than we might think. Although God's provision for all that we need is found in Christ, we will spend our lives learning to believe this is true. The scope of all God has done for us and his true opinion of us can be difficult for us to hang onto.

Since it can seem unbelievable at times, let's rehearse the gospel again. Our sins have been forgiven; God no longer holds them against us. We have been given the righteousness of Christ; in Christ, God has made us perfect forever (Hebrews 10:14). He adopted us into his family and made us his children and heirs. He welcomes us to come boldly into his presence. If we belong to Christ, these things are true of us. God no longer relates to us out of wrath, but as a loving Father. The gospel is hard for us to believe because it seems too good to be true. We are tempted to add something to it. Difficult as it is for us, our part is *not* to add any good works to what Christ has already done, but simply to believe (John 6:29). As we believe that these things are true for us (which is, admittedly, much easier said than done), our faith connects us to the realities behind the words. We begin to see the fruit of the Spirit spring up in our lives, which in my experience is nothing short of amazing.

What Are Your Thoughts?

1. Do you find it hard to get excited about the gospel? Why?

2. What effect has Christ's forgiveness had in your life recently?

3. James 5:16b says, "The prayer of a righteous person has great power as it is working." Cite several specific ways you see this at work in your prayer life. Where are you weak in trusting in Christ's gift of righteousness for you? How has this affected your prayers?

4. Romans 8:32 describes God as a gracious and generous Father. If you approached God with this verse in mind, would the content and frequency of your prayers change? How?

5. Write your own simple summary of the gospel and read it frequently. Ask your Father to work its truth through your life.

Pause and Reset
Faith to Believe

For this reason I bow my knees before the Father, from
whom every family in heaven and on earth is named,
that according to the riches of his glory he may grant
you to be strengthened with power through his Spirit in
your inner being, so that Christ may dwell in your hearts
through faith—that you, being rooted and grounded in
love, may have strength to comprehend with all the saints
what is the breadth and length and height and depth,
and to know the love of Christ that surpasses knowledge,
that you may be filled with all the fullness of God. Now
to him who is able to do far more abundantly than all
that we ask or think, according to the power at work
within us, to him be glory in the church and in Christ
Jesus throughout all generations, forever and ever. Amen.
(Ephesians 3:14–21)

Paul's prayer for the Ephesians opens a hopeful door to us as we work to believe. Some of us do not think of believing as work, but when Jesus was asked what works God required, he gave an unexpected answer that did not reference the commandments or the law. "Jesus answered them, 'This is the work of God, that you believe in him whom he has sent'" (John 6:29).

As we take these words to heart and begin to work at believing, we soon realize that believing is hard work! Sometimes it is hard to believe that our sin is forgiven when it is particularly ugly or repetitive. Sometimes it is hard to believe that the righteousness we hoped would earn us God's favor is filthy rags. Sometimes it is hard to believe that God will receive us with joy when we have failed him yet again. Sometimes it is hard to rely on him when we are competent and in control. Sometimes it is hard to believe that we will ever experience any lasting fruit of righteousness because we are so fickle. We see how easily our attention is diverted from Christ's kingdom work to the pursuit of our own desires. We often fail to believe that we need Jesus; or fail to believe that he will meet us in our need. Much of the Spirit's work in our lives exposes our unbelief, which is hard for us to see, and returns us to the path of believing that the good news is for us.

I have this conversation about the gospel with women in ministry all the time. Everyone's lives are complicated and the idea that believing the gospel will make a difference is hard for us to *believe,* but the transformation can be startling. One woman reluctantly followed her husband into missions, not wanting to leave the charming suburban neighborhood that had been her home. When I first met her, her loss was the primary topic of conversation. But as she began to get hold of the idea that Jesus had done enough to make her right with God as a believer, I noticed that each time we were together our conversations changed from what she had left behind to what God was doing in her heart and in the people around her. By the time she finally returned to the States to live, she could laugh at her attachment to suburbia, because it no longer held much appeal for her. Years of cultivating a heart of belief had changed her values and desires.

We need encouragement to believe the gospel for ourselves, even as we share it with others. The exhausting nature of ministry drags us down and steals our faith. Just one phone call, email, or Facebook posting can ruin our day. Serving people means that we are invested in them; we have intertwined our lives with theirs. Thus, we are vulnerable. Paul's prayer for the Ephesians points us to a source of joy and power that is not connected to our ministry. Rather, it is connected to the character of our Father and the love of our Savior. In his prayer for the Ephesians, Paul prays a prayer we can pray for ourselves.

I learned to pray this prayer at the beginning of our first missionary term in Ireland. I was struggling to adjust to Irish life and culture. It was an extremely difficult transition for our family and the difficulties made me doubt God's goodness and love. The Spirit led me to Ephesians 3 and I began to pray this prayer with great fervor. I would often retreat to our upstairs bathroom and cry through my reading of this passage. Each time I found myself doubting the truth of God's love and care, I asked the Spirit to strengthen my heart so that Christ might be present in me. I knew my faith had to be strengthened so that I could do the work God had called us to do. My confidence today in Christ's love and God's fatherly care for me was forged in the fire of Ephesians 3. In his prayer, Paul reveals the believer's inheritance of joy. If we believe its truths, our lives will be rich with joy. But we need the Spirit to strengthen us to believe in the effectiveness of Christ's work for us.

Paul begins his prayer with the big picture: Look at our God! He points us to God as our Father. As we contemplate the God who gives "according to the riches of his glory" (Ephesians 3:16), our faith will grow. Our Father's giving is big because he is glorious; he is gracious and generous to his children.

Paul then turns his attention to the personal nature of God's love for us. He prays that the Ephesian believers would be "strengthened with power through the Spirit in [their] inner being, so that Christ may dwell in [their] hearts through faith" (vv. 16–17). There are several ideas to lay hold of here. Notice Paul's view that our hearts are weak without the Spirit's power. It isn't natural for us to believe the gospel—it is going to take work! The gospel is counterintuitive to the way the world works, where we must earn whatever we get.

In Romans, Paul explains it this way: "Now to the one who works, his wages are not counted as a gift but as his due. And to the one who does not work but believes in him who justifies the ungodly, his faith is counted as righteousness" (Romans 4:4–5). Our temptation and natural instinct is to add a bit of our own good efforts to Christ's work. This is hard for us to resist. Wages for work is the natural order. Surely we have to do a little something to deserve God's favor! To think that the one who does *not* work is the one who receives God's favor is hard to believe without the Spirit working in us. But the Spirit shows us that when we add our little bit of good work and good intentions to the mix, we subtly push Christ away, refusing to rest in him alone for our standing before God. This is why we need the Spirit's power to hold onto Christ, to trust only in his work for our forgiveness and righteousness.

The Spirit directs our attention away from our performance, which disrupts our faith connection, to look instead at the person and work of Christ. According to Ephesians 3, the Spirit strengthens our hearts to be the dwelling place for Christ. For some of us, this may be a new idea. Christ is so familiar to us that we forget he is the Holy God, the second person of the Trinity. But when we see him as he truly is, he is just too much for us in our frail human state. Without the Spirit working in us, the presence of Christ will overwhelm us—or we will miss him altogether.

On the Mount of Transfiguration, Jesus let some of his glory shine through as he met with Moses and Elijah (Luke 9:28–36).

The disciples were so undone that Peter came up with a plan to build tents in which the holy men could reside. Pitch tents for the holy men? Luke describes Peter's response as "not knowing what he said" (Luke 9:33). A modern description might be "babbling." Clearly, the disciples couldn't grasp what was happening in front of them. Christ's glory does that; his presence overwhelms us. It is hard to comprehend whom we are seeing and what he is doing. Yet the reality is that the risen Christ is at work in us and he is also working through us to gather his people. We need the Spirit's strength to take in both realities.

As the light dawns in us about who Christ is, it begins to make sense that we would be changed simply because we are in his presence. Although he is too big for us to comprehend fully, the Spirit strengthens us to hear his voice and believe what he says. We come to know him, trust him, and let ourselves be loved by him. And love is the key, is it not? The roots of Christ's love work their way deeply into every part of our lives. His love comforts us. His love motivates and changes us. We become grounded in that love. His love is beyond what we can understand with our minds—it "surpasses knowledge," but it is a love we can grow into as Christ makes his home in us. Some of us struggle to believe that his love is for *us*. Ephesians 3 is a wonderful passage to reflect on as we ask the Spirit to convince us that Christ's love *is* for us. The Spirit can do in us what we cannot do for ourselves. He can make us strong and receptive to the presence of Christ, who changes us as he draws us into his deep love.

Paul then takes us a step further to say that being filled with Christ and his love is being filled with "all the fullness of God" (v. 19). How is that possible? In Colossians 1:19, Paul says, "In him [Christ] all the fullness of God was pleased to dwell." The eternal Creator God makes his home in us through his Son. No wonder the Spirit has to strengthen us to be the dwelling place for this God! But if we belong to Christ, this is what the Spirit is doing in us, even now. God has made his home in us. Our problem is the smallness of our imaginations, so Paul pushes us to imagine even greater possibilities of what God can do. No matter how big, wild, crazy, or "out-there" our creative thoughts, God has the ability to do much more.

How out-there can God be? Before the creation of the world, the triune God planned for our redemption. The second person of the Trinity agreed to take on human flesh, which he would then wear for all eternity. This sinless Son would live in a sinful world, surrounded by sinful people, and then give himself as a sacrifice for us. The grave could not contain this holy Son. The Father accepted his perfect sacrifice and brought him back from the dead. He rose with a new, incorruptible, human body as the firstborn of many who will come after him. Jesus became one of us so that we could be included in his family of love.

The point is this: Not only *can* God do more than we could ever ask or imagine—he already *has*! He has revealed his immense love for us. He fills us with himself. I would never have dreamed of any of this, yet Paul tells us that there is still more for us. God works in us with the same power he used to raise Christ from the dead. That resurrection power is at work in us! And it is at work through us to bring others into his family with the same imagination, creativity, love, and glory that conceived our salvation and adoption into his family. The Creator God is at work and he invites us to join in his work of redemption.

What an extraordinary reality Paul presents to us! We are a part of the family of God that spans heaven and earth, and we are all changing to look more and more like our older brother, who is in turn a perfect likeness of the Father. That is who we are! Paul talks a lot about God's power in Ephesians and in this passage particularly. This powerful God is our Father; he works *in* us by his power and *through* us by his power. He strengthens us in our weakness through his Spirit, so that Christ can live within us. His purpose is to fill us to overflowing with his love—a love so big that we need the Spirit's power to grasp it; we need the Spirit's power to retain it. He wants us to be sure of his love. He wants us to know it so deeply that it cannot be taken from us. As we grow in our ability to know his love, we are filled with a deeper understanding of the awesomeness of our God and how we are related to him. We respond to his beauty with love and adoration. We worship.

This passage helps us to see that, on our own, we have only a small view of our salvation. Without the Spirit's work, we cannot absorb the magnitude of God's love for us. We are like ants drinking from a fire hose; our capacity is so small and the water flow so massive that only tiny drops of water go into our mouths. As Ephesians 3 closes with its familiar benediction, we should remember that this benediction is in the context of God's love for us. *Our Father* can do more than we think to ask or even imagine. See what he has already done!

Seeing the power of God's love in a life is amazing. I met a young woman who was agonizing over a decision to go into missions. She was single and felt called to a difficult place. She knew that she would be lonely and isolated and did not want to leave her family behind. But the thing she kept talking about was how much God loved her. She had a rich devotional life and felt certain that God was calling her to do something that was quite beyond her. She ended up making the decision to go, although many counseled her against it. Several years later I saw her on the field and indeed her life was hard, but she was without regret. Although she suffered genuine difficulties and loneliness, her life was also full of unexpected friendships and joy in what she was doing. God's love for her was still the center of her life.

God is calling us to a life in which he will do things in and through us that are beyond our imaginations. As Christ becomes more and more the center of our lives, God's gifts of forgiveness, righteousness, and adoption have transformative power. Our faith grows stronger as we connect with Christ's love for us. Through the gospel we see glimpses of God's beauty and the glory of his kingdom work. These glimpses help us to let go of our expectations and agendas and open ourselves to what he is doing. As our confidence grows in God's love for us, our creative thoughts grow bigger and our prayers become bolder for the people we pray for and for Christ's kingdom to move forward. Yet even then we will have barely scratched the surface of his power at work in us.

As these truths sink deeper into our hearts, the gospel works boldness in us to step into the world with less concern for ourselves. Becoming more certain of God's love strengthens our faith. Experiencing forgiveness and the cleansing of our conscience as we regularly bring our sins to Christ works real change in us. Although we may find it hard to believe at times, God's willingness to sacrifice his Son for us reveals the high cost he was willing to pay to make us his children and the value he places on us. As we believe afresh each day in the work of Christ for us, our trust deepens in our God, who will not stop loving us.

Chapter 4
A Split-Level on the Battlefront

*Battlefront: the region or line upon which
opposing armies engage in combat; the area in which
opponents or opposing ideas meet. (Wiktionary)*

BEING IN MINISTRY places us in a battle for our faith and the faith of others. Although our battlefront may look as innocent as a church building, it is littered with casualties. Those who have never worked in a church may view our war analogy as melodramatic. After all, our churches are full of good people and often located in nice neighborhoods. Yet the church is the frontline of battle for Christ's kingdom. All who work in the church—pastors and their families, youth workers, worship leaders, women's ministry leaders, Christian education directors, etc.—live in harm's way and feel the effects of the battle. The difficulties of ministry are real and many have fallen. We all know stories of adultery and secret sins, children who have left the faith, and burn-out, just to name a few. Only our connection with Christ will sustain us for the long haul.

The first section of this chapter will focus on the unique pressures of pastors' wives, although many of their experiences are common to all women in vocational ministry. These unique pressures begin early. I first met a woman who is now my dear friend when her husband interviewed for a church-planting internship at our church. She accompanied him to a local Chinese restaurant, where Josiah and I met them for dinner. She was beautifully dressed in a light-colored outfit. I had no idea at the time how nervous she was. Near the beginning of the meal, my friend spilled soy sauce on her dress—a lot of soy sauce. It was a minor moment for everyone else, but God's gift to her. When she returned from a fruitless effort to remove the stain, she was more relaxed and a little freer to be herself. After all, what else could she do? The evidence of her imperfection was there for all to see.

Working in the church puts enormous pressure on us to be competent and "together." The pressure my friend felt was real as she attempted to make a good impression for her husband's sake. Every pastor's wife knows that she can disqualify her husband for a job. As we go through the interview process with our husbands and then enter the world of the church, we never lose the sense that we are being scrutinized, no matter how gracious the church leadership. We are married to the pastor, so it is naive to think that our words and actions will have no consequence. Of course there are expectations of us! If you suspect that there is an unwritten job description by which you are being measured, it is probably because there *is* one and you are feeling its effects. The pressures we all feel as we enter church ministry are real, but often invisible to everyone else.

The traditions, roles, and expectations we encounter are often ambiguous and vary from place to place, but their effect on us is largely the same. We are expected to negotiate church life with grace. The role of pastor's wife can be confusing. Although Christ has placed us with our husbands in the church for ministry, we are often treated as free labor to fill in wherever needed. Some of us have become competent free labor, while others of us find ourselves making excuses to disengage. Although many of us have been taught that our role as a pastor's wife is something in which we can excel and take pride, a growing number of women with more modern sensibilities rebel at these roles. They feel that since they are not being paid, they should be free to pursue a life that isn't tied to the ministry of the church. Our varied efforts to cope with the pressures of ministry may reflect our confusion about Christ's call to us. Yet his call to pastors' wives is just as real as his call to our husbands. He doesn't call one without the other. We can trust him to lead and guide us. Our interaction with the church will reflect the uniqueness of our personalities and gifts, our time of life, our health, and our jobs or careers outside the home. Christ does not have a checklist of duties for pastors' wives and he desires us to be strong enough to resist the checklists of others. Jesus is not grading us; he is leading us. As we grow in our experience of God's love and acceptance, we will step into ministry with less fear and duty and more faith and joy.

As different as our individual lives may be, pastors' wives cannot escape the reality that we have an impact on our husband's ministry. It may seem unfair, but our attitudes about the church and our response to people set a tone for the ministry we have with our husbands. Some common examples are the responses people expect from us. They assume that the pastor's wife will be friendly and glad to see them. People appreciate it if we know their names and enough about them to carry on a decent conversation. In a larger church, we may not know that someone has lost a job, but people count on a sympathetic, caring response when they tell us the news. They hope that we will care enough to stop and pray with them. We have been given a position of influence that can be used for ministry. Our responses and attitudes have an impact.

Our lives are full of phone calls and message taking. We receive emails, texts, Facebook messages, and tweets in an all-access world.

We need to manage these communications with grace. Always letting our phone go to voice mail makes people feel we are too important to answer their calls. Forgetting to return a call or deliver a message can be hurtful if someone needs help. Being abrupt on the phone with someone in difficulty is harsh and uncaring even if we are having a tough day and they have called repeatedly. Using Facebook or blogs to vent our frustrations is selfish and foolish and will come back to haunt us. When folks connect with us, though they are not aware of it, *they expect us to reflect Christ's love to them* even in something as mundane as a phone call. These are just a few of the expectations placed on us.

We should not be surprised when people ask us personal questions. Handling random, often inaccurate comments about us or about our husbands is just a part of life on the frontline. Many times we cannot defend ourselves because the reasons for our actions or words are confidential. People often misjudge us because they don't have all the facts. Perhaps the most pertinent question for pastors' wives is not "What are our spiritual gifts?" but "Do we have some grit?" We will not last long in ministry if we spend our time correcting inaccuracies. Christ's good opinion of us is the anchor that will hold when the waters get rough.

The access people have to our lives involves us in the lifelong task of self-monitoring. Have you ever met a church member in the grocery store who checked out the contents of your shopping cart? I have. Then comes the moment of panic when we wonder whether we should explain why we are buying gourmet cheese or rib-eye steaks. Or have you argued with your husband in the hardware store and looked up to see a couple from church staring your way? I have. "Oh no, what did they hear? Do we need to explain why we are not *really* arguing about which electrical socket to buy?" These moments are so common that most of us monitor ourselves automatically. Our ministry radar is constantly looking for potential land mines. Successful monitoring keeps our limbs intact.

Church culture recommends vanilla with sprinkle of spice as the perfect flavor for a pastor's wife—interesting and quirky, just not *too* interesting and quirky. Church folk tend to think of us as somehow belonging to them, and want to take pride in us. This pride manifests itself in a myriad of ways. We might be congratulated for homeschooling our kids and staying quietly in the background. Perhaps people love our community involvement and the active role we take in the public school. Maybe our hospitality and open home get us noticed. Today, as our culture continues to shift, we may be valued for our successful career outside the church.

Most women are intuitive and read expectations well. Our husbands may be blissfully unaware of the pressures we feel, but we sense what flavor we are expected to be. Should we spice up or tone down? Recently, someone made a comment to me about a pastor's wife who, she felt, dressed too well. I was surprised that this friend had such prejudices. Can you identify? We all have examples of the assumptions people make about the pastor's wife. People's expectations can easily overwhelm or annoy us. Because of the great pressure they are under, even our pastor husbands may be the source of much of the pressure we feel to lead, participate, and meet expectations. When they confuse our performance with their reputations, we will feel lonely and unsupported. Our husbands are sinners too, and do not always lead us into a faith response to Christ. If we are not standing on the firm ground of Christ's work of salvation we will be crushed by the expectations that daily surround us.

Shall I continue with some of the expectations that pastors' wives encounter? We should be kind even when we know people are using us for access to our husbands. We should respond with grace when criticized. Or—the oddest and most awkward of all— we should think it perfectly normal to have our husband's salary and value debated in a meeting with us present. We have entered a world where our relationships have shifted. One friend, a relatively new pastor's wife, was perplexed that she and her husband were not included in the social activities of couples their age. Although she saw these folk as equals, they did not reciprocate. The reality of ministry is that people view us differently. Sometimes the shift is barely perceptible, but more often than not, people around us will not relate to us *normally* anymore.

To counteract this tension, there is a trend, especially among younger church planters, to say that pastors' wives are no different from anyone else in the church. They are just members of the congregation. There is an obstinate determination to make it so! Because we live in a society that is aggressively fair-minded, we believe that fairness dictates that we should be free to do what we want, even if we are married to the pastor. After all, our husbands were hired for the job, not us. Many of us prefer to think of ourselves as just another volunteer. Shouldn't we be free to decide how much, if any, ministry we want to pursue?

This determination to resist any predetermined role is no more helpful than striving to fulfill an idealized one. Neither reflects the reality of our situation. Whether we like it or not, people look to us as an example of the gospel at work. The confusion we feel when our expectations (we are just like everyone else) do not match our experience (people look to us as an example) often results in depression, bitterness, disengagement, and a hard edge to our personalities after years of coping. I have had the privilege of speaking with many pastors' wives and these are common responses to the stress of church work. How could it be any other way? It is unhelpful and untrue to think that the pastor's wife is just like everyone else, regardless of how much we wish it to be so.

Even while we trust Christ to work through us, we may have to navigate difficulties without much outside support. We learn to be vague about our lives so that we are not constantly explaining ourselves. Often we cannot tell people why we are discouraged or having a bad day. Sometimes it is our circumstances and sometimes it is our sin, but usually it is not something we can talk about. (For example, I found out today that a church member has been cheating on his wife, or I am angry with a deacon who is making my husband's life miserable.) The average church member has no idea of the layers of information and relationships we manage. And we are not free to share it.

These are some of the challenges and struggles of a pastor's wife. It's better to have a realistic view of these things. There is no virtue in being ignorant of our situations. The temptation, however, as the complexities of our lives intensify, is to shift into management overdrive or throw up our hands in surrender. These may appear to be our only options, but Christ has something else in mind. Regardless of the opinions of those around us, he did not call us to be the church go-to girl. Jesus has called us to spiritual ministry. Whether we recognize it or not, the sincerity of our relationship with Christ will have a deep effect on the life of the church. Wherever our ministry is focused, outwardly in our communities, quietly behind the scenes, or more up-front and visible, people will be affected by the genuineness of our relationship with Christ.

This changes everything about the way we view ourselves. "Doing" is put aside. We no longer judge our impact simply by what we do. But some may say, "I like doing. It's manageable. Bring on the to-do list!" We have a hospitality ministry. We lead a Bible study. We teach Sunday school. We make meals for shut-ins. We are part of the prayer chain. These are quantifiable contributions. At least we are seen doing something! When someone asks about our involvement, we have a legitimate answer. But it is this simplistic view that gets us into trouble. It does not address all the layers of life that we daily navigate. We can *do ministry* without giving ourselves to others. We can hide behind activities and keep ourselves safe, but a busy life full of doing is not spiritual ministry. Christ has more for us.

Some of us serve in very traditional, conservative settings while others of us rock out on Sunday morning in our blue jeans. The funny thing is that no matter where we serve, many of us do not exactly fit the situation in which we find ourselves. If we are at the blue jeans church, perhaps we would like to dress up and sing hymns occasionally. Or perhaps those in traditional settings might long for more freedom in their worship times. We have all seen the poster with four adjoining fields and four cows craning their necks to eat the grass in the field next door. We are those cows! The grass in the next field always seems more desirable. Working in a church long term is difficult, and we often use the awkwardness of our *fit* ("If I were just living in that green field over there . . .") to let ourselves off the hook.

Those in ministry are in a unique position to deeply affect the life of the church. It is hard for us to believe that we are the ones Christ will use to move his kingdom forward (especially if we are always looking for a greener field), but *we* are the ones he has called. Believing that he has purposefully chosen us for the situation we find ourselves in will free us from the *duty* of ministry to see the *joy* of its possibilities and the prospect of enjoying the grass in our own field. If you find yourself saying yes to most of the requests asked of you, you are probably responding to the expectations of those around you. If you find yourself saying no to most of the requests asked of you, you are probably reacting to the expectations of those around you. Knowing that we have our Father's approval will keep us from being crushed and manipulated by others' expectations. We will be able to say yes and no from a place of freedom and faith. Every time we feel the weight of those expectations we should run to our Father for help. His approval silences others' opinions and our own noisy consciences so that we can respond to the Spirit's leading each day. Women who give themselves for the gospel in a church environment are the kingdom's unsung heroes. I love and admire these amazing women!

What Are Your Thoughts?

1. Whether you are paid for your ministry position or married to the guy who gets the paycheck, in what ways do you define your worth by what you do?

2. No matter where you serve, how do you feel about the idea that yours is a spiritual ministry?

3. Where have you avoided genuine engagement in your ministry situation?

4. In what areas do you resent God's call on your life?

5. In what areas of your life have you seen thankfulness change your attitude?

6. What insights about yourself can you glean from your answers to questions 1–5? How would you like to see God change you?

Pause and Reset
Thirst

On the last day of the feast, the great day, Jesus stood up and cried out, "If anyone thirsts, let him come to me and drink. Whoever believes in me, as the Scripture has said, 'Out of his heart will flow rivers of living water.'" Now this he said about the Spirit, whom those who believed in him were to receive. (John 7:37–39a)

The temptation for those who serve in churches is to get so busy or weighted down by life that we forget to enjoy Christ or offer him to those around us. Surrounded by so many options and opportunities to fill our time or overwhelmed with just getting through the day, we can ignore the work that the Spirit really wants to do in and through us. We are naturally occupied with family, church, work, and friends. Even though we are called to open our doors to the world God loves, we often miss those moments because we have too much to do or are just plain tired. Ministering in the familiar can lull us into comfortable routines we can manage quite apart from the Spirit. Our struggles to cope can fill our thoughts and keep our focus on ourselves. We forget what we are about.

Whether we are married or single, ministering on campus or in a church, our home culture carries with it significant danger. Because we are surrounded by so many resources, both Christian and material, we can be blinded to our need for Christ. The constant press of people can cloud our vision. Although we live in a spiritual desert, we are often unaware that we need the water that only Christ can give, and we miss his voice when he asks, "Are you thirsty for my presence today?" We are too busy coping and managing life. But when we realize our thirst for Christ, he promises to more than quench it; he promises rivers of his Spirit flowing through our lives. His description of the relationship he wants us to have with him is very different from the safe and managed lives that many of us settle for.

When I returned to the States to resume life as a pastor's wife after eight years in Ireland, I found reentry into my home culture difficult. Don't get me wrong: I am thankful for my "magic" blue American passport when my foot hits American soil because it is the one time I experience a hassle-free welcome into a country. American citizenship is an enormous blessing. I feel safe here in a way I never do anywhere else in the world. After a long flight, standing in the line designated for U.S. citizens at passport control is always the moment when I know that I am home.

Returning to America after a long absence gives unique perspectives on both its strengths (my sigh of relief at the airport) and weaknesses. I had forgotten, for example, how much money and effort people put into their leisure activities. These pursuits were a constant topic of conversation, which made me feel out of sync with those around me. Making strategic financial decisions to ensure a comfortable standard of living was another major topic of conversation. Josiah joked that when we left Ireland, we were flush—that is, we did not owe anything and we did not own anything. We had more in common with those who were twenty-something than we did with the folks our age. Returning to the States often pushed me to fear and worry as I heard phrases such as "your investments," "your portfolio," "your savings," "your safety net," and "your retirement" over and over.

Just as confusing were the solutions American culture offers to deal with the stress and strain of life. We are encouraged to indulge ourselves with everything from spa days to darker, richer chocolate. It is no wonder that Christians may not feel a thirst for Jesus—culturally speaking, we have too many drink options available to artificially quench our thirst.

Sometimes the deep needs revealed in us through the rigors of ministry push us to Christ—we know chocolate and a massage won't be enough! This can result in times of great encouragement and comfort that make us willing to persevere. Still, even here, our culture (including our Christian subculture) offers many temptations to turn elsewhere to meet the needs we have. Books and downtime, conferences and counselors are all ways we try to manage the stress that ministry brings. The help we find there, as well as the camaraderie of others in ministry, can offer real encouragement to us, but even these good things won't be enough to quench our thirst for Christ or make us a conduit for his Spirit.

Those in missions may feel this thirst for Christ more quickly and keenly. (Having done both kinds of ministry, I identify with both.) With the trappings of a familiar culture removed, missionaries can feel needy just navigating the everyday. But those who work in a foreign culture face a great temptation as well. It takes a strong individual to get to the field, and relying on that strength is a daily temptation for missionaries. There aren't many cultural supports for missionaries to rely on. Self-sufficiency is a natural consequence. Missionaries are a resourceful group who get things done. The downside is that even though we may feel our thirst, we can go a long time before we take a drink.

Crossing an ocean does nothing to smooth out the deep ruts of sin in our lives. The coping skills we had in our home culture will be creatively adapted into our new one. We may be free from the outward indulgences of our home culture, but if we haven't learned to go to Jesus with our thirst, we will still be stuck with the same self-reliant, self-indulgent hearts that learn new ways to satisfy themselves.

Regardless of the ministry we are involved in, whether we live at home or abroad, Jesus's offer of "rivers of living water" is hard for us to believe. Many of us are tired and discouraged, frustrated and lonely, but we still avoid admitting our thirst for as long as possible. In fact, we may not see our struggles as thirst at all. And when we finally admit that we need help, our independent natures lead us to quench our thirst by redoubling our efforts, self-medicating, or managing things better. We forget that Jesus is the only one who can meet our need. Even when we remember, we may find it so hard to believe Jesus's offer *for ourselves* that we walk away. It can't be that easy! Those rivers can't be meant for us! Rivers of water flow by our feet, but we are unwilling to bend low and take a drink.

Others of us struggle to believe and see little evidence of these rivers in our lives. We are believers, but our living water has been reduced to a trickle. Perhaps we never had much of a flow at all. We may find ourselves in ministry because of our husband or other influences rather than our own call from God. When these rivers of the Spirit are absent from our lives, we naturally assume that Christ's offer is not true or that we have somehow missed our opportunity. It's either God's fault or ours if those rivers are not flowing from us. What else could it be?

Actually, our questions and failures create a door of opportunity for us. Our weaknesses can become our strengths because they reveal our need; they turn our focus from ourselves to Christ

(2 Corinthians 12:10b). Of course, we can choose to remain weak. We can say that the trickle is all there is for us. Weakness does not magically turn into strength.

But Jesus's offer to the thirsty gives us insight into how our weaknesses can make us strong. If we are willing, our weaknesses, struggles, and failures can be the flash points that awaken us to our need for Christ. When weakness reveals our thirst and we go to Christ, he responds with rivers of living water, an overflow of his Spirit. When Jesus quenches our thirst with his Spirit, our weaknesses have become our best friends because they remind us of our inability to do anything apart from Christ. Leaning into our strengths, gifts, and abilities creates an illusion of spiritual competence, but leaning into our weaknesses grounds us in our need for the Spirit to produce lasting fruit in and through us. We then agree with Paul: "For the sake of Christ, then, I am content with weaknesses, insults, hardships, persecutions, and calamities. For when I am weak, then I am strong" (2 Corinthians 12:10).

One dear friend who has been in ministry for many years models these ideas well. She is a high introvert who often hosts long-term guests. She also consistently volunteers to cook for and host events. All these activities are draining, but she does them with genuine joy and grace. Knowing her weaknesses well, she schedules occasional alone time to renew and regroup. Instead of using her people-exhaustion as an excuse to say no to ministry, like Paul, she glories in her weaknesses. This friend regularly puts herself in situations where she knows she will feel her need for Jesus so that ministry does not become something that she does apart from the Spirit.

I have another friend who is an amazing doer. Energetic and efficient she can get more done in a day than I can even think of to do. Her work is a great help to those in need. Yet she has made teaching the Bible a high priority in her life. Although the results have been slow compared to her high-efficiency days, she has seen the fruit of spending a large chunk of her time studying and teaching Scripture. Doing comes naturally to her. Taking time to work through Scripture with women who are unbelievers or new believers keeps her dependent on the Spirit. She doesn't feel her need of Christ so much when she is organizing things, but each time she meets with the women in her Bible study, she is keenly aware that only the Spirit can open their eyes and hearts to the gospel.

These women habitually put themselves in situations where they are weak and will feel their need for Christ. You do not need to convince them that they are thirsty as ministry drains them dry. Although they are normal women with normal struggles, they have learned over the years that only Christ can renew and refill them when they start to feel empty. Still, for many of us—and even for these faithful women at times—we forget Christ's promise that if we will come to him with our need, he will fill us to overflowing with his Spirit. Sometimes we are full of pride in our accomplishments; at other times we are discouraged by our inadequacies or lack of results. Jesus's voice is easily lost in the din of battle. Yet his message to all of us, whether we are tough or fearful, managerial or disorganized, competent or frustrated, is simple. He invites us to come to him. Being needy is a normal result of spiritual ministry, since we are giving what we cannot renew in ourselves. Our need for renewal pushes us back to Christ. Many times we do not recognize our thirst, but just as when someone hands us a glass of cold water and we say, "I had no idea how thirsty I was!" so is the moment of being in Christ's presence. We become aware of our thirst even as he fills our glass and, as water begins to spill over onto the floor, we realize we have water to share.

Jesus promises rivers of his Spirit pouring through our lives. In the middle of church and kids, language learning and bureaucracy, homework and dogs, grocery stores, oil changes and the millions of other things that fill our lives, Jesus tells us that rivers of his Spirit will flow through us. We have odd ideas about what that looks like so we often miss the wonder of it in our daily lives. The Spirit's flow through our lives is the love, joy, peace, patience, kindness, goodness, gentleness, and self-control he creates in us to bless those around us. It is the boldness to speak to others about this Jesus we are learning to love and depend on. His Spirit takes us beyond what is comfortable to places we would not naturally go to share Christ. Faith does not presume that the flow of God's Spirit will be predictable and always look the same, but believes that when we come to Jesus with our thirst, the rivers of his Spirit will flow from our hearts to the places he wants those rivers to go.

I experienced a wonderful example of the unpredictability of the Spirit's flow as we traveled around the country raising support to return to missions. In each new city we had to find places to meet our everyday needs. For my haircuts and highlights I would choose a salon for its proximity. I never knew what the results would be. You may know that highlights take a couple of hours during which your foiled hair is wild and frizzed and all dignity is set aside. One day I walked into a small salon with two stylists and one other customer. I took my seat, and as usual, began to chat with the stylist. That day the conversation quickly became one of the most amazing conversations I have ever had about Jesus.

The woman was an older divorcée who was new to the area and had recently become a Christian. She had no Christian background and knew little about the Bible. The second stylist, finished with his customer, sat down to listen to our conversation. For two hours no one came into the shop and—frizz, foils, and all—I talked about the work of Christ with a passion and clarity that was obviously of the Spirit. It was one of those rare occasions where you hear yourself speaking but know that it isn't really you. Both stylists (one a new believer, one not) were captivated by the gospel. They had heard about church Christianity but never about the work of Christ for those who believe. I left the salon full of joy and utterly amazed at what the Spirit does through us at the most unexpected times and in the most unexpected places. I have no memory of my appearance when I left the salon that day!

The Spirit flows through our everyday lives, and sometimes the results are extraordinary. Faith opens our eyes to the work that God is doing. This is how we "keep in step with the Spirit" (Galatians 5:25). And when ministry begins to drain us and we feel thirsty and needy, we know where to be renewed and refilled. We come to Jesus with our thirst and leave confident that as rivers of his Spirit are flowing through our lives, we will be filled with his love for us and his love for the world.

> O the deep, deep love of Jesus, vast unmeasured,
>   boundless, free!
> Rolling as a might ocean in its fullness over me!
> Underneath me, all around me, is the current of Thy
>   love.[3]

Chapter 5

Those Awesome Missionaries

Awesome: causing awe or terror;
inspiring wonder or excitement. Colloquial: excellent,
exciting, remarkable. (Wiktionary)

AMONG WOMEN IN ministry, if those working in churches are on the front line of battle, then missionaries are the ones who "take the hill." We move to foreign places to capture new territory for Christ. As with those in stateside ministry, sometimes missionaries are put on pedestals and sometimes the unique challenges we face are simply ignored. Someone once asked movie star and dancer Ginger Rogers what it was like for her to dance with the great Fred Astaire. I love her answer! She said that she had to dance every step as well as he—just backwards and in heels. And so it is with the missionary. Missionaries do many of the things that other women in ministry do, but in a foreign culture and often in a foreign language.

When we entered missions after twelve years of church planting, we noticed that people treated us differently. My husband, who had been well connected in our denomination, suddenly was unable to get pastors he knew to return his phone calls. He was no longer a peer—he was raising support. He had just turned forty and was told by many that he was having a midlife crisis, not called to be a missionary. As we began to raise support, sometimes we were treated like spiritual heroes, which was embarrassing and inaccurate. At other times we were treated like hired workers assigned to bring activities designed to entertain a room full of preschoolers. Although *Lucky Charms* and St. Patrick Day kitsch had nothing to do with our work in Ireland, I always had a box filled with each in the trunk of our car.

Josiah and I used to joke that missionaries are at both the top and the bottom of the Christian food chain. People think that those who actually sell their houses and cars to answer Christ's call to missions are at the top of the spiritual food chain, which is why many struggle to see missionaries as normal people who feel the losses of our calling. A woman once told me that she could never leave her family and move overseas because her family was close and really liked each other. She assumed that family was not important to me otherwise I would not be able to leave them. Yet practically, when it comes to raising support, missionaries magically fall to the bottom. Often homeless people—and I mean no disrespect to the needs of the homeless—have an easier time getting through the doors of the church for money than a missionary does.

In the previous chapter I highlighted many of the pressures and difficulties faced by those in direct church ministry and I hope I created quite a bit of sympathy for them. Although I have never been on a church staff, having been a pastor's wife for many years has given me access to the extensive challenges faced by everyone involved in church work. A tough faith and a soft heart are helpful prerequisites. In this chapter, we will begin by looking at the unique dynamics felt by missionary women, both single and married. In my experience, the Christian community struggles in its response to missionaries. The pendulum swings between "superheroes" and "just like us—we are all missionaries" neither of which is accurate. Until we stop thinking of missionaries as awesome superheroes or odd people who are always asking for money, we will be unable to grasp the reality of their lives, which can encourage and strengthen the church to lift its eyes from itself to the fields that are "white for harvest" (John 4:35). Appreciating the consequences that missionaries experience because of the gifts and calling God gives them will help the church to listen to their unique perspective and love them well.

What is life like for those who are called to missions? The challenges of missionary life are difficult to generalize. Those in European cities find that people have little interest in the gospel. Europeans are generally secularists who think that Christianity has run its course. Many African countries are open to the gospel, but are terribly hard places to live in. Much time and energy are spent on everyday survival. Asian cultures have particularly difficult languages and their open idol worship creates an oppressively evil atmosphere. Those in countries dominated by a state religion are not allowed the free speech that most of us take for granted. Many missionaries struggle just to stay well. In this big world, no two places are quite the same.

Living outside the States as a missionary has many challenges. Setting up a household, finding schools, buying vehicles, sorting utilities, and navigating government requirements can be crazy hard overseas. To make matters worse, often these tasks must be done in a language the missionary is only beginning to learn. Simply choosing what to put into the shipping container requires a degree in logistics. Getting a driver's license is often an expensive nightmare that involves mandatory driving lessons and the learning of road rules that make no sense to us, and which we forget during our driving test. Permission to reside in a country is an ongoing hassle with paperwork, trips to government offices, and changing requirements that only come to light when we fail to meet them.

It's a humbling experience to stand in line at the alien office to ask permission to stay another year in our chosen country. Before I had this experience, I assumed that every country would be glad for me, as an American, to reside within their borders. The missionary quickly learns that this is not the case.

While our legal status is being negotiated, we also face the challenge of learning a new culture and in most places a new language. Mothers often struggle most with language learning because they can't put aside the care of their children. A missionary wife once told me that she had become accustomed to missing much of what was going on around her, even though she had made great strides in language and cultural learning. It was clear that the Spirit had worked a deep patience and humility in her through her situation. The world is extremely varied, but no matter where missionaries live, they navigate pressures and difficulties beyond what they would experience at home. The grace that missionaries need is often for tangible things like dealing with arbitrary government officials and functioning with unreliable power grids or enduring the humiliation of language learning and the isolation of never quite belonging. They need grace to persevere in a world that can no longer be relied upon to go according to plan.

Practically speaking, there is something to be said for the competence and efficiency America affords us. When life runs smoothly we get more done, have more time for people, and more time to enjoy the good things God gives us. But overseas, plans have to be negotiated over and over again. Efficiency and competence can no longer be relied upon. From cooking with what is available to opening a bank account to communicating with locals, everything has to be learned—and when we think we have learned it all, we realize that we have just begun. After three years in Ireland, Josiah commented to an Irish fellow that he had progressed in his understanding of Irish culture just enough to realize that he did not know what was going on at all. The gentleman replied that it was the first time he had heard an American admit what the Irish knew all along. There are no shortcuts to the time required to learn how to communicate the gospel to those in a different context. Missionaries must relinquish speed and efficiency and take the long view.

Missionaries go to Mexico and Malaysia, Siberia and South Sudan. Whether single or married, with or without children, all face obstacles. Few who have not lived as missionaries can grasp the complexity of such a life, which is why missionaries need the faithful prayer and loving support of believers and churches back home. In turn, missionaries give the church the names and faces of a wider world that needs Jesus, which helps keep the church's vision from becoming inward and self-serving.

Living overseas changes those of us who are missionaries. When we return to the States we are often experienced as a peculiar group of people as we struggle to reenter the church cultures we left behind. We see the world differently because of our experiences. Our old culture no longer fits us anymore. And while all believers need Jesus, missionaries can often appear to need Jesus more than most. We are not usually at our best when we return home, and this can be reflected in our frustration at the church's use of its resources, our frantic pace to visit everyone we have missed, and the difficulty we face to sum up years of work in a Sunday school class or "missionary minute" during a worship service. Missionaries can be boring speakers as we talk of people no one knows and get excited about things that don't seem exciting. Because missionaries already feel overwhelmed when they return home, it takes creativity for the church to access the unique gifts the missionary brings to the church and, at the same time, love them well.

The Spirit's call to ministry is unique for each of us. Yet, for missionary women, that path will include hardships that are different from the hardships women called to their home culture experience. Yet, despite those hardships, missionaries are some of the sanest and most fulfilled women I know. Our understanding of our gospel calling translates into selling our possessions and packing our bags. The missionary's call to leave our home culture is experienced amid the overflow of grace God promises to give when we need it. His grace gets us on the plane. His grace keeps us in country. I will never forget waiting in the Atlanta airport with our teens to fly to Ireland and thinking, "What in the world are we doing?" The neediness we feel pushes us to ask for that grace often. This creates a unique dynamic for the missionary. The promises of Christ are often the most tangible resource the missionary has. I love my missionary sisters!

While we all should have great respect for the pioneer spirits of missionary women, we need to be clear that the impetus to leave familiar comforts for the unknown is a gift from the Holy Spirit. It may be a gift to be desired and can be a gift for which to pray, but the passion that the Holy Spirit works in us that takes us from our home culture is not because we are the choicest candidates. It is not a gift we manufacture or deserve. It is a gift. Those who have received it find that life in our home culture does not bring satisfaction. There is a longing to take the gospel to those who live at the ends of the earth. Jerusalem, Judea, and Samaria hold little appeal for us (Acts 1:8).

Regardless of where God has placed us, all of ministry is a battle. If you are in ministry, this is something you already know. We are daily surrounded by casualties; often, we are among them. If we are going to be effective participants and not bodies on the field, we need to understand the subtle and not-so-subtle ways we are tripped up, derailed, and mesmerized by our enemies—the world, the flesh, and the Devil. Even as the church is God's vehicle of movement into the world, so a sinner who has been forgiven and made righteous is his instrument. God uses us his people to communicate his good news to the world, so it is not surprising that we are under attack. We don't often think this way, but it explains why we so easily forget our need for Christ and his provision for us. Since God uses his children to bring the message of his Son to the world, it is imperative that we know that message for ourselves. We need to fight with intentionality so that we are not among the casualties. We fight to believe the gospel for ourselves so that we may encourage others in their believing.

If you are not a missionary, you may be feeling inferior as you imagine missionary life, but if you do, it is only because you forget that God provides special grace for his unique call to missionaries. Those in missions do not have the grace needed to be a pastor's wife (unless they are missionary pastors' wives!) or to work in the convoluted culture of the church. And only those who serve in parachurch organizations are given the special grace they need to pour themselves into the lives of students and those they serve. It is a funny thing. Personally, I had more freedom as a missionary although everyday life was much harder. As a pastor's wife I had much less personal freedom, but life in general was much easier. My friends in parachurch organizations often struggle with the subcultures of those organizations, which have their own unique set of rules and expectations. All women in ministry have their hands full! We will only grow in our ability to love and encourage each other when we appreciate the grace God has worked in all of us who lay down our lives for the gospel whether in our home country or in a far-off place.

However, this is not always our response. This world system, our flesh, and the Devil himself tempt us to respond to ministry hardships by forgetting what Christ has done and trusting ourselves to manage life as best we can. The stress of ministry pushes us to many ways of coping regardless of where we live. Some of us eat to comfort ourselves—I am guilty of that. Some of us watch feel-good movies for comfort—I am guilty of that. Some of us work out for an endorphin boost—I am sometimes guilty of that. Some of us go shopping to feel better—I am guilty of that. Some of us get lost in the pages of a book or surf the web to forget our troubles—

I am guilty of that. And I believe that all of us have found relief from the strain of ministry by comparing ourselves with other ministry women who, we feel, have not performed as well as we have or sacrificed as much. Nothing cheers us quite as easily as comparing ourselves with those who somehow make us look better and feel more spiritual. I am guilty of that. From what I've seen in my own heart and observed about others, this may be the unconscious coping strategy for many women in ministry. We naturally compare ourselves with others to feel better about ourselves.

I once read about a woman who grew up in a poor rural area. Her mother took in ironing to earn money and, as the girl grew up, she began to iron with her mother. She continued into adulthood and made ironing her life's profession. She did not earn much money, but decided to live simply so that she could save. Each week she deposited a meager amount of money into a savings account. After many years, her savings had grown to such an extent that she could begin doing what she had dreamed of all along. She gave educational scholarships to poor young women who wanted to go to college.

There are several things about this story that I find amazing. When this woman tells her story, you instantly realize that she is a happy person. She does not grieve her lack of opportunities. She never married. She did not spend money on herself, even as the world began to change. She never updated her humble little house. She ate simply. She was full of joy for the good she was able to do for others and felt it the privilege of her life that she *had the money* to give.

The Spirit reminds me of this woman from time to time. She exuded thankfulness. She felt deeply called. She lived quietly and anonymously and was completely humble when her giving and her secret calling were revealed. She did not think of herself as anyone special. She was genuinely thankful for the opportunity to give others the college education she was never able to have.

It is easy for us to compare ourselves with others. Is the ministry of the senior pastor's wife more important than the ministry of the youth minister's wife? Is the single missionary whose time is fully focused on ministry more valuable than the missionary mother who spends most of her time caring for her children? Is a woman serving in a place of physical hardship more spiritual than the one serving in a modern city? Are missionaries in general more committed than those who choose to stay at home? Are teaching gifts more valuable than hospitality gifts? Do women on the worship team add more to the service than women who make the coffee?

We fall into the temptation of judging the way the world judges. We look at our impact. We think about our sphere of influence. We look at our abilities and analyze our resources. We measure our sacrifices. We make a judgment. From this worldly viewpoint of comparison, we may wind up despising where God places us and discontent with the resources has supplied. As we experience the hardships and confusion of ministry, we may question God's fairness. We wonder why we are in it and we disconnect. We convince ourselves that if our circumstances were different or we had different abilities and better gifts or a more exciting calling, we would pursue ministry wholeheartedly.

There are many roles in which women serve in ministry. Many are in support roles, such as pastors' wives and some missionary wives, while others are in primary ministry positions. Some of us serve in our home cultures and others launch out into the unknown. Regardless, we are all tempted to compare ourselves with others. We cannot seem to help ourselves. Yet there will always be those who outshine us. They may be kinder or more gifted, braver or better educated, more loving or serving in a harder place, in better shape or more intelligent, more faithful or better looking, fantastic cooks or more comfortable in their own skins, healthier or better able to recall Scripture and (when circumstances require it) there are some who appear to leap tall buildings in a single bound. But if we measure ourselves with other women in ministry, we will be today's ministry casualties. Both pride and discouragement separate us from Christ.

We all struggle with similar issues. Women who are single and in ministry, whether longing to be married or content in their singleness, experience pressures and difficulties without a human companion. As we fight to stay connected to our husband, we who arc married evoke the line from Dickens's *A Tale of Two Cities:* "It was the best of times, it was the worst of times." If our lives include children, trying to care for them in the midst of ministry will take us on an emotional journey filled with life's highest highs and lowest lows. These experiences happen no matter where God has placed us or how we serve.

God gave me a wonderful gift in the story of the woman who ironed. I am prone to comparing myself with others, but there is no comparing myself with this woman. I find her story deeply affecting. I want her confidence in her calling. I want her humility. I want her heart, which is content with what God gives and overflows with thanksgiving and joy. When we can rejoice in who God has made us to be and where he has placed us, our focus shifts from who is working in the hardest place, doing the hardest job with the most enviable gifts to *all* being deeply valued. There are no superwomen in the kingdom of God. Even if some of us can jump pretty high.

What Are Your Thoughts?

1. Do you feel that your ministry is more or less valuable than others? How so or why not?

2. Do you find yourself negotiating with God for different gifts and circumstances? What do you wish were different and why?

3. How do you feel about the statement, "There are no superwomen in God's kingdom"?

4. With whom do you compare yourself? How does that affect your opinion of yourself and your ministry?

5. What gives us the ability to mentor and be mentored without comparison (which always results in pride or discouragement) intruding itself into our relationships?

Pause and Reset
Contentment

For by the grace given to me I say to everyone among you not to think of [herself] more highly than [she] ought to think, but to think with sober judgment, each according to the measure of faith that God has assigned. For as in one body we have many members, and the members do not all have the same function, so we, though many, are one body in Christ, and individually members of one another. Having gifts that differ according to the grace given to us, let us use them: if prophecy, in proportion to our faith; if service, in our serving; the one who teaches, in [her] teaching; the one who exhorts, in [her] exhortation; the one who contributes, in generosity; the one who leads, with zeal; the one who does acts of mercy, with cheerfulness.

Let love be genuine. Abhor what is evil; hold fast to what is good. Love one another with [sisterly] affection. Outdo one another in showing honor. Do not be slothful in zeal, be fervent in spirit, serve the Lord. Rejoice in hope, be patient in tribulation, be constant in prayer. Contribute to the needs of the saints and seek to show hospitality.

Bless those who persecute you; bless and do not curse them. Rejoice with those who rejoice, weep with those who weep. Live in harmony with one another. Do not be haughty, but associate with the lowly. Never be wise in your own sight. Repay no one evil for evil, but give thought to do what is honorable in the sight of all. If possible, so far as it depends on you, live peaceably with all. Beloved, never avenge yourselves, but leave it to the wrath of God, for it is written, "Vengeance is mine, I will repay, says the Lord." To the contrary, "if your enemy is hungry, feed him; if he is thirsty, give him something to drink; for by so doing you will heap burning coals on his head." Do not be overcome by evil, but overcome evil with good. (Romans 12:3–21) (The word "sisterly" was substituted for "brotherly" to highlight the inclusion of all in the text.)

Romans 12 is particularly helpful for the ministry life into which we have been called because it describes a servant of Christ. Although these words are written to every believer, as those in ministry, we lead as Christ leads. We serve and lay down our lives for others, and this passage gives us insight into what it looks like for us to lead in this way. As we ponder it, we need to remind ourselves that ministry is the work of the Spirit, flowing from a life centered on Christ. We misinterpret this passage if we use it as a yardstick to measure our own efforts. The coming of Christ changed all that, but we can easily return to self-effort to commend ourselves to God. Until we die or Jesus returns, we are stuck with a sin nature that is convinced it can please God. If we forget that we are bent to sin in this fundamental way, we will alternate between pride and despair as we succeed and fail to measure up to passages like this one. But Christ has paid the penalty for our sin and fulfilled the law for us, so we can approach this passage with a prayerful expectation that the Spirit will show us what he wants us to see. We can hear what he has to say to us without fear. Christ is for us and we are safe in his love. This passage is full of promise and the power of the Spirit at work in us.

Paul begins by explaining why he is able to give such specific and pointed directions. He does so because of the grace that has been given to him. He gives us a clue as to how this works when he writes, "Having gifts that differ according to the grace given to us, let us use them" (Romans 12:6a). As he boldly exercises his gift of exhortation, we realize the large measure of grace he has been given. He begins by simply telling us not to think more highly of ourselves than we ought, but to take stock of ourselves in light of the faith we have been given. If you are confident of your gifts, this might seem like a reasonable way to start the conversation, but if you are unsure of your place in the body, this may feel like a tough beginning. Hang in there; Paul has words of encouragement for all. Since we are part of one body, our individuality is essential to the whole. Everyone has a place and a call. Paul says we have all been given gifts to serve others and the faith to use them.

Even as this passage speaks of the wide diversity among God's people, its message has a great leveling effect. We do not get to choose our gifts. When we are thinking rightly about ourselves (not too highly), we understand that the measure of grace we are given for the gifts we are given is all from God to affect his ends. He does what he wants, with whom he wants, how he wants, when he wants, and where he wants. This can rub us the wrong way if we have too high an opinion of ourselves. The Spirit's work is to reorient us to the reality of God as King. This is no small thing but is the core of our rebellion. We want to be God. We want to be in charge of the gifts we are given and how we use them. Only as we allow the cross to level us with everyone else will the ministry described in this passage take place. Even the way God organizes his kingdom work humbles us. He chooses who gets what gifts in what measure. This is hard for us. We want some credit for our dedication and sacrifices, but Paul says that even our pursuit of Christ and his kingdom is according to the measure of grace given to us.

Why are these ideas so important to grasp? If we aren't convinced that all good gifts come from God *as* gifts and that the source of all grace is the finished work of Christ, we will fall prey to the idea that we somehow earn God's gifts by our devotion and commitment. Our experience of his grace and gifts will somehow make us feel superior to those with lesser gifts and weaker faith or inferior to those with greater gifts and stronger faith. When we forget that we all need the blood of Christ and his righteousness, a sense of entitlement creeps in to pollute our fellowship with Christ and the power of the Spirit's work.

Paul does not intend us to read this passage as a ministry checklist or a critique of what we lack. If we read it that way, we will be defeated before we begin as we respond in pride or despair. Rather, this passage is full of hope and promise for those who trust in Christ. He gives gifts to his children and faith to his children. His call to serve is also a promise to give us all we need to respond. This passage is a promise of the gifts and fruit that the Spirit will produce in and through us. No one has every gift, but God gives us the gifts we need. Then he gives us the faith we need to use them.

If we read this passage as a list of accomplishments we then can use to compare ourselves with others, we think too highly of ourselves. We think that being the person described in the passage is within our reach. It is not. If we read this passage and are filled with discouragement, it is *also* because we think too highly of ourselves. We think it would be within our reach *if we could just get it together.* It is not. This passage is not a scorecard for successful life and ministry. It is God's promise to his people to provide everything we need to follow him. In the everyday press of ministry, this passage brings hope that God is at work, providing the gifts we need for this day and giving gifts to those he has called us to shepherd and love.

As we read Romans 12 with faith, we begin to get excited about what God is doing and how we are part of it. We see the many ways he works and the diverse people he uses. Our hope rests in his power and his willingness to make us into the humble, loving, generous, and faithful people Paul describes to bless his church and expand his kingdom. When we are willing to rejoice in the gifts God has given us, we will be free to rejoice in the gifts he has given others. As long as we compare ourselves with others, we will quench the Spirit with our pride or with our fearful unbelief. But as we realize that it is up to God to distribute his gifts, pride is replaced by humility and fear is replaced by courage as we step out in faith. We can be at peace with what he has assigned us and get busy living out of what he has given.

John Milton wrote: "They also serve who only stand and wait."[4] In his forties, Milton was devastated by blindness. Through his suffering, he learned a great truth: simply standing in God's presence is a worthwhile, glorious calling. Our culture teaches that those who want to be recognized must distinguish themselves from the rest and we often import this idea into the spiritual realm. But God is not like that. He has a place for each of us in his kingdom. He is thoughtful in what he chooses for us. We don't have to distinguish ourselves from others to get his attention. Sometimes he asks us to wait and sometimes we can hardly keep up with him. But, knowing that God carefully chooses his gifts to us and promises to provide the faith we need to use them, we can take Paul's words to heart and be content: "Having gifts that differ according to the grace given to us, let us use them" (Romans 12:6a).

Chapter 6

The Tangle of Culture and Ministry

Tangle: to become mixed together or intertwined;
to be forced into some kind of situation; to catch and hold.
(Wiktionary)

THOSE OF US who have never left our home culture probably don't think a lot about its influence over us. We don't have to leave our native land to encounter different cultures however. The American melting pot is always adding new cultures to blend in and add new flavors to the mix. Living in Louisiana introduced me to a culture very different from the one in which I had been raised. During our missionary training, we were assigned to live in inner city Detroit and work in a Spanish Baptist church. Both of these places had cultures that were foreign to me. Moving to Ireland was a more drastic cultural shift for our family. Most of us in ministry leave familiar cultures and learn to live in new ones.

To communicate the gospel clearly in the places we live, we must recognize how our home cultures have influenced our opinions and worldview. Otherwise, we will inadvertently mix our cultural preferences and prejudices with the teachings of Christ. This was startlingly evident to me on a visit to Uganda, where Josiah was privileged to speak to the Presbyterian Church of Uganda's general assembly. A female missionary friend and I were invited as honored guests to this normally all-male event. One thing that struck me particularly was that the men wore coats and ties. Now, Uganda is on the equator and it is always hot and sticky. There is no air conditioning and few fans. Yet these pastors had long ago adopted a habit of coats and ties because they modeled themselves after missionaries and visiting pastors who wore coats and ties when they preached. Although Scripture does not teach us what those who proclaim God's Word should wear, we often export our Western traditions. I'm sure that the missionaries of years past did not view their Western expressions of Christianity as additions to Scripture, but they were, and they resulted in a dress code for many Ugandan pastors.

As I have visited churches around the world, I have seen such incongruous bits of Western culture in many worship services. On that same trip to Uganda, we had a worship service with Ugandan and American college students. The Ugandan students led worship with a keyboard and song selections imitating worship tapes they had been given. Frankly, the music was not very good. Yet earlier I had heard those same students' amazing musical abilities with drums and voices. No one had instructed them to lead worship with a keyboard, but they were eager to please their American visitors. Perhaps they were unaware of the value of their own cultural expressions of worship. The Western church has exported a style of worship that requires money and equipment. In some instances our worship style is included as part of the gospel message we communicate as we instruct new believers on how to *do church*.

I have participated in many ministry moments that were negatively impacted by culture. It's going to happen because culture can't be avoided. We cannot live above or outside culture. It provides our worldview and basic orientation. We dress, eat, recreate, and form relationships conforming to its norms. We have to wear something. We have to eat something. We have to spend time doing something. We all need relationships and community to survive. Our cultures provide convenient, logical solutions to our needs.

There is good in every culture because each mirrors the Creator in some way. But since people are sinners, each culture also reflects the sins and biases of its people. Recognizing where our cultural prejudices impede gospel communication will enable us to present the gospel more clearly. Disentangling ourselves from old prejudices and loyalties is a skill we need to develop, so that culture becomes a tool for ministry rather than a hindrance. When we can recognize the cultural particulars that shape our identity and learn the cultures we enter as Christ's messengers, our message will be truer to Scripture. For those of us who have grown up in the church, thinking through our cultural biases can be particularly challenging because culture and Scripture have been jumbled together for us. It is natural for us to read our cultural values into Scripture.

One obvious example is how the evangelical church of the American South is identified with political conservatism. To many outside the church, the gospel of Christ has been reduced to a political agenda. It was the same in Ireland. In the early 1990s, to be Irish was to be Catholic. The two were inseparable. As Irish believers learn to be Irish followers of Christ without the religious and political baggage of Irish culture, they have a significant impact. It is the same for all of us.

Paul described his movement into other cultures this way: "I have become all things to all people, that by all means I might save some. I do it all for the sake of the gospel, that I may share with them in its blessings" (1 Corinthians 9:22b–23). Many believers from Jewish backgrounds were unhappy with Paul's message and methods. They wanted Gentile converts to conform to the laws and regulations that had characterized God's people before the coming of Christ. Paul had to regularly defend himself against their accusations of compromising and erratic behavior.

What were Paul's responses to these cultural issues as he took the gospel to the Gentiles? Sometimes Paul circumcised those who were with him and sometimes he refused (Galatians 2:3–6). Was Paul compromising the gospel message? He ate meat offered to idols with some and abstained with others. Was he inconsistent in his practice? Paul saw these issues as cultural biases that needed to be confronted to avoid confusing the gospel with the traditions and practices of both Jews and Gentiles. His decisions reflected his desire to communicate the gospel in a way that kept its message clear and pure. Paul wanted to be clear that salvation is a free gift from God to all who believe in his Son—*apart* from circumcision and Old Testament requirements of the Law. Christ's coming changed everything and Paul was adamant that his daily choices would reflect that change. Paul entered many cultures during his missionary journeys and in his letters we learn how he conveyed the gospel to each one.

I was raised in the southern United States. Although the South has many flaws and has changed over the years, I am thankful for my roots and enjoy many things about southern culture. I like the way people in the South are generally friendly and polite. We open doors for each other, and say "Excuse me" when we bump into someone. We refrain from rudeness while driving and, when provoked, feel a need to call our mothers to apologize for our failure. We are hospitable. We keep our speech at a moderate pitch and consider loud voices in public intrusive and tacky—except when we are laughing and telling stories. We tell lots of stories and frequently make fun of ourselves. Most southerners enjoy irony and fill our conversations with our many idioms. The Irish used to get a kick out of our southern idioms ("That dog won't hunt"; "Even a blind hog finds an acorn every once in a while," to cite two). Few in the South miss a regular gathering of faith without a twinge of guilt. The South is all about family and faith, food and conversation, taking time to enjoy life and, of course, music. Buddy Holly, Elvis, and Johnny Cash are our sons; Dolly, Loretta, and Aretha, our folk heroes. Our southern identities are expressed by men with names like Muddy Waters and The Blind Boys of Alabama and made famous by the likes of Louis Armstrong and B.B. King. And, of course, who hasn't heard Lynyrd Skynyrd sing, "Sweet Home Alabama"? The South would not be the South without her music. Outsiders often consider our culture fake, but it is a true expression of our values. I've learned that whether I intend it or not, I bring my southern culture with me wherever I go.

Why talk so much about my culture? I am deeply influenced by it just as you are deeply influenced by yours. Without a clear idea of the cultural values we hold dear, we unknowingly tangle them with Christ's teachings. I heard about a pastor from New England who was called to a church in Mississippi and vowed not to waste money on air conditioning for Sunday services. There was no such waste of God's resources in his previous church! It did not take long for him to realize that few would be attending his un-air-conditioned church in Mississippi. Summers in Mississippi are a bit warmer than summers in New England, and his cultural bias did not translate well to his new situation.

I have made many cultural missteps as well. During our first Christmas in Ireland, I devised a plan to get to know our neighbors. I assembled a group of Christmas carolers and made bread to leave at every house we visited. I worked hard to make the evening a success and we prayed earnestly for God to bless it, yet the evening was a fiasco. What I failed to account for was the role of carolers in Irish culture. Carolers collected money for charities. So when we arrived at each house singing our carols, everyone tried to give us a coin. As we politely refused the coin and gave them a loaf of bread with our perky, "Happy Christmas! We are your neighbors!" they were genuinely stunned. Later, a neighbor's daughter told me that her mother was angry because she did not have a gift for us in return for our loaf of bread. By her standards, it made her look bad. (The following year we did not attempt caroling. This same mother renewed her anger toward us because she had purchased a gift for us in anticipation of our return. When we did not show, she was stuck with a gift she later sent us, via her daughter, to let me know she did not appreciate our unpredictable behavior.) Not long after our night of caroling, we received several tins of cookies from neighbors who felt obligated to pay us back but never spoke to us again.

If I had been living in Alabama, my plan would have been brilliant: friendly carolers with lovely banana bread. But it was a disaster we never quite recovered from in Dublin. We do not know what we do not know. That's why we must acknowledge our continuing need for cultural education. Our ignorance and assumptions affect our ability to connect with people when we unknowingly offend and confuse them in our attempts to have gospel conversations.

Another experience came after we had been in Ireland for about a year. My errands one day included a trip to the shops for food. Finally learning the Irish names and pronunciations for the meats I wanted to purchase gave me a sense of confidence as I placed my order with the butcher. He finished his work and handed over my packages. I offered my thanks, turned to go, and was answered with a booming Irish-Gomer Pyle accent, "Y'all come back now, hear!" I was stunned. I was mortified. Was that how I sounded to everyone? I did not turn to look at him as my face flushed with embarrassment. My dignity and confidence were in tatters as I slunk to the checkout. I had no idea that what I considered a slight southern accent was Gomer Pyle to Irish ears.

But here is the interesting part. Because I was still lagging behind on the nuances and cues of Irish culture, what I thought was the world's most embarrassing moment was actually a moment of acceptance. After coming to the meat counter for a year, the Irish butcher was paying me a compliment by "slagging" me. In Irish culture, slagging is a way to say that you are one of us. Only friends slag friends; outsiders are not worth the bother. With his biting humor, he was letting me know that I was now accepted as a local shopper. I was no longer an invisible outsider. Had I understood this, I could have scored major points with him by responding with a "Hey y'all—thanks" in an equally exaggerated southern drawl. This would have probably gotten a laugh and improved my chances for future conversations. It took me a long time to recognize the opportunity I had missed that day.

We will make cultural missteps as we carry the gospel to unfamiliar places. There is no getting around it. My caroling idea was supposed to give our neighbors a good opinion of us and smooth the path for future gospel conversations, but it was simply not a good idea. The connection I failed to make with the butcher because I mistook friendliness for rudeness was never recovered. Misreading that encounter revealed my cultural ignorance *and* how deeply my southern value for *niceness* affected my experiences. Southern children are not told to be good when we leave the house, we are told to be nice. After years of living in a culture filled with *nice* people, I misunderstood a relational opportunity that came my way because it did not feel nice to me.

We soon learn that there are up sides and down sides to all cultures. There are cultural moments we get and others that never make sense to us. The point is not that one culture is superior to another, but that effective gospel communication requires learning new cultures. We must be willing to leave the familiar to be, for a time, uncomfortable and unsure of ourselves. Taking the gospel *to* people means that we enter their world rather than inviting them into ours, which is no small thing.

The challenge of entering a new culture often has a subtext we may not see. The cultural biases that have shaped us not only confuse our interaction with new cultures, they also entangle and blind us to repetitive sin patterns from our old culture. Many of these patterns have deep roots because they tap into cultural preferences that seem fundamentally right to us. I had no idea how my southern value for niceness colored my responses to people and situations. My desire for things to be nice was frequently at the heart of my complaints against God as well as my attempts to control others. Our cultural biases can be fertile ground in which our sin takes root and flourishes. It's good to be aware of it.

What was sinful about my caroling idea that first Christmas? Wouldn't it be more accurate to say it was unwise or ignorant? I was certainly ignorant of the culture and clearly made an unwise decision, but there is always much more happening under the surface in these moments.

American missionaries labor under an enormous weight of culture—and we bring it with us. When Josiah and our colleague Hunter went to Dublin city center to meet up with an Irish fellow they had never met, they were surprised when he approached them on the street and introduced himself. "How did you know it was us?" they asked. "Ah, that one is easy; you Americans walk like you own the street." This eureka moment took on mythic proportions for our team. It explained so many of the struggles, confusions, and failures we had in our efforts to connect with the Irish. None of us had any idea that this cultural arrogance (to which we were blind) was such an enormous hindrance to our gospel communication. It was the beginning of a complete change in the way our team did ministry, although it by no means solved all of our struggles or cured our arrogance.

My caroling failure was an innocent error in one way, but it had a big impact on our ability to enter our neighbors' lives. The American arrogance with which this nice southern girl made ministry decisions had an impact. My need to get going and do something we could write about in a prayer letter had an effect, but it was not a positive one.

This brings to mind another aspect of American culture that has a huge influence on us. America is a society that values and excels at efficiency. The temptation to evaluate our every breath from this vantage point is powerful. How does our commitment to efficiency affect ministry? First (and not insignificantly), supporters of our churches and our mission work often judge our effectiveness by the results we produce, so we are constantly tempted to shade the truth, finagle the numbers, and invent every sort of creative response to give supporters and folks in our congregations the answers they want to hear—that we are making measurable progress.

Our personal interactions with those we serve also can be deeply affected by our love of efficiency. We may become frustrated and angry with people who slow us down or proud when we get things done well and quickly. We might find ourselves discouraged when we don't produce at the rate we think we should. We might criticize others who don't work as hard or as smart as we do. We may pray perfunctory prayers or forget to pray at all before we make our plans because subconsciously we're sure that our abilities and ideas will bear fruit. We frequently judge our impact by how many items we can check off our list rather than how well we love those around us. Efficiency is a cultural value that encourages many of us to judge, criticize, lie, boast, rely on ourselves, disregard the weak, and respond with irritation and frustration to those who don't share our love of efficiency. It colors our relationships and ministry decisions more than we might think.

The convoluted sin patterns we struggle with make ministry challenging enough, but when you add our self-confident, efficiency-oriented, can-do culture into the mix, it is truly miraculous that God's kingdom moves forward through us at all! American culture is not unique in that way; every culture has sinful values that impede the gospel's progress. But the glory of Christ and his resurrection power become clearer to us when we realize that he uses culturally-biased, forgiven sinners to spread his good news around the world.

What Are Your Thoughts?

1. Describe your home culture.

2. What are some specific cultural values that have affected your view of God? How do they affect your ministry?

3. If you are living in a culture other than your own, how have you learned to communicate the gospel differently?

4. Try reading through the description of your home culture with the eyes of an outsider. Do you see yourself differently?

5. Paul describes his ministry as becoming all things to all men. How are you adapting to those around you so that they might have a better understanding of the gospel? Where can you improve?

Pause and Reset

Surrender

So if there is any encouragement in Christ, any comfort from love, any participation in the Spirit, any affection and sympathy, complete my joy by being of the same mind, having the same love, being in full accord and of one mind. Do nothing from selfish ambition or conceit, but in humility count others more significant than yourselves. Let each of you look not only to his own interests, but also to the interests of others. Have this mind among yourselves, which is yours in Christ Jesus, who, though he was in the form of God, did not count equality with God a thing to be grasped, but emptied himself, by taking the form of a servant, being born in the likeness of men. And being found in human form, he humbled himself by becoming obedient to the point of death, even death on a cross. Therefore God has highly exalted him and bestowed on him the name that is above every name, so that at the name of Jesus every knee should bow, in heaven and on earth and under the earth, and every tongue confess that Jesus Christ is Lord, to the glory of God the Father. (Philippians 2:1–11)

As the Spirit works in us, our insights and ideas about taking the gospel *to* people will continue to grow. Even stateside, culture can be a challenge. Our churches reflect ethnic cultures, economic cultures, age-group cultures, music cultures, denominational cultures, urban cultures, West Coast cultures, East Coast cultures. The list is long. Even going across town to a different neighborhood might require us to cross cultures.

Jesus understands what it means to cross culture. He left the joys of heaven to come to earth. In heaven he was known and worshiped. The Gospels chronicle how he was treated when he left heaven to bring salvation to us. Leaving the place where we are known, valued, and understood is a common experience as we follow Christ. We go where he takes us. We leave things behind. He reminds us to not look back at the things we surrendered to follow him.

Following Christ should turn our worlds upside down, but our loyalties to our cultures and the ideas they have fostered in us are deep. Losing all to gain Christ includes leaving behind those loyalties and cherished ideas when they conflict with our loyalty to Christ and the teachings of Scripture. Leaving these things behind is not automatic; many of us unknowingly hang on to them.

One cherished cultural ideal is our high value for social equality. It is difficult to untangle from this. Truly, this desire for the equality of each citizen reflects what is best about our country; it is something for which we should give thanks. But as women who are believers, our society's pursuit of equality may get tangled with our reading of Scripture. Our Western viewpoint can and often does affect our response to the New Testament teaching on the authority and leadership of men in the church. (See 1 Corinthians 11:2–16; 14:33–35; Ephesians 5:22–24; 1 Timothy 2:8–15; Titus 1:5–9; 1 Peter 3:1–6.) Because we are bright, talented, and gifted women, the limited ministry opportunities available to us may breed dissatisfaction in us. They do not correspond to the leadership opportunities we have in society. Saying that God's thoughts are not our thoughts and God's ways are not our ways (Isaiah 55:8) in regard to this issue is an understatement indeed. And when our reasoning is based on our cultural values, we will not understand God's wisdom or ways. We will continue to look back at the "equality" we left behind.

"Have this mind among yourselves, which is yours in Christ Jesus, who, though he was in the form of God, did not count equality with God a thing to be grasped, but emptied himself, taking the form of a servant, being born in the likeness of men" (Philippians 2:5–7). One day I bumped into a woman from our church at the grocery store. I had not seen her in a while and she informed me that she was no longer attending because our church did not allow women elders. She was angry that God was allowed to be a male chauvinist and she had little respect for me because she felt that I, as a woman, should be standing up for the right of women elders in our church. For more than an hour we leaned on our grocery carts while I talked with her about the Christ of Philippians 2, who, though equal with the Father, made himself nothing for our sakes. Before our conversation, she had assumed that my views on the role of women in the church came from my traditions. Afterwards, she may not have agreed with me, but she knew my opinions were based on my understanding of Scripture.

Many Western women have been distracted and wounded by God's organization of his church. Why do men get spiritual authority that women do not? If we cannot answer these questions for ourselves, surely we will be ineffective as we disciple and encourage women, particularly younger ones, who expect the church to reflect their cultural values.

Just as other cultural baggage muddles our communication of the gospel, so our ambivalence and reluctance to embrace the New Testament teachings about women will not help us in ministry. Christ never intended his church to be a democracy. Our displeasure at men's spiritual authority over women shows our confusion in our reading of Scripture. This colors our communication of the gospel. Throwing out the writings of Paul that exasperate us because they no longer reflect society's values reveals how little we understand the nature of the God whom we worship. It will not help us bring Christ to the nations. If we don't want our cultural presuppositions to influence our representation of Christ's life and work, the Spirit needs to change our minds and our loyalties in all areas of life.

There are many ways that the Holy Spirit changes our minds and realigns our loyalties. Sometimes he reveals more of God's holiness. This awakens us to our deep need, even as believers, for a Savior. The love God has for us becomes personal when we think of what Jesus did for us. His love has a powerful effect as it finds its way into our hearts. His love changes us and we defer to his way of thinking.

I knew a woman on a church staff whose ideas were never taken seriously, even though she was gifted in ministry. Her heart had hardened by the time she had a fresh encounter with the gospel. When she began to see large areas of sin in her own life, her bitterness at the way she was treated began to fade. As she began to pray for others' success and promote their ideas, her opportunities for ministry in the church became more than she could handle. The humility God worked in her took her from the sidelines into the heart of ministry. When she stopped fighting for position and authority, she got her heart's desire: to be a part of the real ministry of the church. As we grapple with the roles assigned to women

101

and men in the church, remembering Jesus's sacrifice will keep our hearts tender and open to God's way of doing things. As Christ's followers, we might be helped to look more carefully at the values of the One we are following, outlined in the second chapter of Philippians.

Before considering the passage from a woman's viewpoint, it might be helpful to remember that the passage was also written to men. We can read it in light of men's responsibilities to lead the church. Paul never encouraged leaders he trained to lead from a position of power and strength or to lord their authority over others (2 Corinthians 1:24). Even in their leadership at home, Paul requires husbands to "love your wives, as Christ loved the church and gave himself up for her" (Ephesians 5:25). Christ taught men to lead as he led. Christ washed feet. Christ became a servant. Christ gave his life for us. Christ loved sacrificially. The leadership he requires is nothing like the leadership we find in the world. Christ never condones ego, arrogance, or an authoritarian dictatorship, even if it is benign.

Christ's requirement for humility in men is no less than it is for women. Having the heart of a servant is just as hard for men as it is for women. Women are naive if we think it is easier for men to carry the authority of church leadership as servants than it is for women to submit to that authority as servants. Servant-leadership is just as foreign an idea in our culture as the idea that modern women would willingly place themselves under male authority. As we take Christ to the world, we will bring a false gospel if both women and men do not reflect the humility of Christ described in Philippians 2.

Although women are equal with men in every way (Galatians 3:28), we are asked to take a subordinate role in regard to spiritual authority in the church. Christ was also asked to take a subordinate role to provide for our salvation even though he was fully equal with the Father. For a time he left behind all of the authority and honor due him in order to become our Savior. In Christ's choice to step down from heaven, he experienced deep suffering.

We hear one night of his suffering described in Hebrews: "In the days of his flesh, Jesus offered up prayers and supplications, with loud cries and tears, to him who was able to save him from death, and he was heard because of his reverence. Although he was a son, he learned obedience through what he suffered. And being made perfect, he became the source of eternal salvation to all who obey him" (Hebrews 5:7–9).

The suffering described in Hebrews 5 took place on the night before his crucifixion. The second person of the Trinity was brought low. For his time on earth, Jesus set aside his equality with the Father and the glories of heaven. That night in the garden he was reduced to loud cries and tears to be spared a death he did not deserve. He suffered. We have no way of knowing how deeply Jesus suffered, yet out of his night of suffering came an obedient yes to the cross. His humiliation and sufferings bought our salvation. As we suffer the humiliation of our roles and treatment at times, we can find comfort from an understanding Savior, with encouragement and hope that God will use our suffering for our good and for the good of his kingdom.

I was recently at a church planters' conference, staffing a Serge booth with a young male colleague. As the morning progressed, we were amazed and then amused that not one of the church planters who approached the booth talked with me or even glanced my way. I was completely invisible to them. It was striking how those young men assumed that an older woman of average appearance could not have anything worthwhile or helpful to say to them.

This is a small, but I think, significant example of the way women in ministry can be slighted. Christ has given gifts and abilities to women as well as men. We all have his Spirit. We all reflect his beauty and glory and have insights into his Word and how that Word can be communicated to those around us. But many men assume that we women have little experience or spiritual depth to offer them. It is true (for which I'm thankful) that many of us are under humble church leadership that values our gifts and abilities, but most women in ministry have had these moments of invisibility. We serve in an imperfect evangelical culture that can really push our buttons. My tenderhearted husband confesses that he can be a real jerk at times. In my experience, many men I have met in church leadership could join in his confession. Yet women are still asked to submit to men's authority in the church.

Jesus was fully equal with God the Father but took a subordinate role to redeem us. This role brought him humiliation and suffering. Do we think that our suffering in the subordinate role that Scripture outlines for women in the church is somehow greater than his? The question may feel hard-edged, but it is the question we must answer as we consider Jesus's response to his role in salvation's plan. One of the beauties of being a woman is that we image Christ in this way. Many of us do not understand it and few of us like it. We struggle, sometimes with loud cries and tears, as we experience injustices and slights. But if we are willing to give up our democratic opinions and identify with Jesus, we will see the honored role God has given us. We can find joy that we are counted worthy to imitate Jesus by taking this subordinate role in the church for our time on earth, just as he submitted himself to the will of the Father. Like Christ in the garden, we can learn obedience through our suffering.

Many times we want to be followers of Christ without actually having to follow him. We want to choose when and how and where we will go. We want to choose what we will believe about God and what we will change. We want to be in charge of our discipleship so that it fits our preferences and plans. But these are not choices that followers are free to make. Followers follow. Will we follow Christ down the road of humility and be humbled, or will we go the way that fits with our sensibilities and keeps our pride intact?

Christ did not grasp his position of honor and authority, but took on human form. Comparatively, this Holy God emptied himself. He became a servant. Each day he was a man was a deeply humbling experience for the Son of God, and his humiliation culminated in being killed by sinful men. This perfect Christ became the sacrifice for the sins of those who mocked and killed him. "For our sake he made him to be sin who knew no sin, so that in him we might become the righteousness of God" (2 Corinthians 5:21).

This is the Savior we follow—the God who gave himself completely for us. There is hope for us as we stand in the presence of the risen and reigning Christ who once made himself nothing because he loves us. Are we willing to be encouraged and comforted by him in our struggles and suffering? As we allow Paul's Philippians 2 description of Christ to penetrate our defenses, how can we refuse the comfort of our God who left the honor and joys of heaven for us?

Often we do not understand why Jesus does things the way he does. Our cultural prejudices, invisible to us, cloud our perceptions. Frequently, God helps us along in our understanding but at other times, Christ steps into our confusion not with answers but with a reminder of the cost of following him. "To another he said, 'Follow me.' But he said, 'Lord, let me first go and bury my father.' And Jesus said to him, 'Leave the dead to bury their own dead. But as for you, go and proclaim the kingdom of God'" (Luke 9:59–60). Some of us want to get everything in our lives organized and nailed down before we follow Christ, like this man who wanted to stay behind and bury his father. Others of us don't bother to seriously count the cost of following Christ before we start our journey down the road of faith (Luke 14:25–33).

In ministry it is easy to organize our lives around activities and people without addressing the internal loyalties we must renounce to follow Jesus. We may not realize the cost until the Spirit disrupts our way of thinking through Scripture or circumstances. The cost of following Christ may look differently as we get older. After almost fifty years as a believer, I am still discovering new things I must leave behind to follow him. Yet God is faithful and full of mercy. As we follow, his Spirit teaches us what we must leave behind for the sake of the gospel and frees us to let go of it.

Following Christ is a lifelong journey that happens day by day. Our bias toward our cultures and our wrong ideas about Christ and his kingdom are not revealed to us all at once. Each day we read Scripture; each day we pray; each day we ask the Spirit to reveal our sinful thoughts, actions, and allegiances; and each day Jesus teaches us new things about himself and his kingdom and we learn to trust him more.

Jesus knows it is difficult for us as Western women to step onto the unknown road of ministry. Where will he take us? What if we do not want to go where he leads us? If we submit to his ways, will we become invisible? As women, our cultural values of equality pull us away from Christ and weaken us. We waste a lot of time, energy, and opportunity worrying over things we should have left behind. Jesus understands our struggles as women. Although he empathizes with us in ways that might surprise us, his call to us remains constant: "You, follow me."

There is a popular song "Waste" by *Foster the People*[5] in which a young man's love for a girl is revealed by his willingness to bear her deep weaknesses as he patiently waits for her to want to change. It is a beautiful description of love and reminds me of Jesus's patient love for us women who have been whipsawed by our culture and cannot decide which way to turn with our trust. Many of us waste much of our lives unwilling to wake from the values of our culture. We don't want the changes that come from giving ourselves completely to Christ. The honest but patient love represented in this song is a dim reflection of Christ's love for us. Jesus will not give up on us as he waits for us to want the changes that result from giving ourselves unreservedly to him.

Jesus is committed to those he loves. He became one of us so that he could lay down his life for us and make us his own. We cannot shake him or get rid of him when his views or requests are inconvenient. He speaks; he waits; he woos us. He is empathetic with our wrestling because he too wrestled with God's plan. He is not impatient in his pursuit, but shows a love beyond our imagining as he waits for us to catch up with him. If we choose to waste the riches of his love and grace, we can. If we persist in our refusal to believe that the gospel will actually change us, we can. And if we want to waste this day in a pride that requires him to conform to our prejudices before we serve him, he will let us waste it. He is faithful even when we are not and he will not let us go. When we say no to him, we miss much of what is amazing, fulfilling, enlightening, comforting, wonderful, and hopeful about belonging to him—but we still belong to him.

As his love works on our hearts, we will grow dissatisfied with our selfish choices. His love awakens us from our sleep to the reality of his kingdom coming. He helps us see who he is and what he is doing in this world, and he draws us into his plans. And as we see his kingdom coming, our desires begin to change. We want to be more like him. Jesus changes us into those who are not grasping equality, but willingly take the place of a servant. Through our suffering we learn his humility and begin to reflect his beauty. We benefit from the changes he makes in us, but these changes are never for us alone. In his kingdom the Savior becomes a servant, the Word (John 1:1) becomes a baby, and we too give away our rights so that others may know him.

Paul's description of Christ in Philippians 2 also gives us the end of the story. Although Christ was made low for his time on earth, after his resurrection he was exalted to a place of honor. All will bow the knee to him in worship one day. All will confess his Lordship for the glory of the Father. We too suffer as we follow Christ, but only for a season. Jesus will raise us up one day and we, both women and men, will reign with him forever.

The more time I spend reading the Gospels, the more I realize how completely different God is from me. Jesus is not manipulated or fooled by our cultural biases any more than he was influenced by the biases of his day. He will not be moved to support our prejudices. He just will not budge! Much of the resistance and frustration we feel is because we are working at cross-purposes with him.

When we judge the quality of our lives by our culture's values, we will always be dissatisfied. Being a servant, taking the low place, and esteeming others as better than ourselves makes us grumpy and irritable—if we forget that Christ made himself nothing for us. We enjoy talking about God's upside-down kingdom, but we do not like the upside-down way it works with our equality.

In the church, humbling ourselves under the leadership of men may be one of the hardest things women do, particularly if we are competent leaders ourselves. The leadership out there is often uninspiring, but when we are angry or discouraged we can spend time in Philippians 2. The Spirit will draw us into the life of Christ and his sacrifice for us. There we understand that our response to him is not about the quality of the human leadership over us. Jesus experienced bad leadership and authoritarian rule as the Son of God, but he did not fight for place or reputation. Instead, he humbled himself. He really is nothing like us in our pride, but he invites us to become more like him in his humility.

Chapter 7

Fair Is a Four-Letter Word

Four-letter word: a reference to any of several of the strongest English swearwords that are also four letters long; any words considered to be taboo in a given scenario (regardless of how many letters). (Wiktionary)

WE WILL NOT always experience fair treatment in ministry. Many of us have had seasons of life when "That's not fair!" was our constant refrain. We often find the double standards and unrealistic expectations of others hard to cope with. "That's not fair!" may run through our thoughts more often than we realize. Expecting fair treatment from those we serve can be extremely unhelpful for women in ministry. Our expectations set us up for disappointment, and, before you know it, "fair" becomes an expletive in our vocabulary. Don't get us going on the unfair way we have been treated! Most of us could probably talk about it for a long time.

Fairness is not bad. Just as equality is a wonderful value as people interact with one another, fairness has the same effect. It is better on everyone when fairness is held in high esteem. We teach our children the importance of fairness in playing games and sports.

We go to bat for those who are treated unfairly. These justice issues are at the heart of many of our ministries. The office of deacon was created in the New Testament because the Hellenist (Greek) widows complained that the Hebrew widows got preferential treatment (Acts 6:1). The church is the one place where everyone should expect that the rich are not preferred over the poor or the powerful over the weak. We rightly work for fairness for others, yet our commitment to our own fair treatment as we follow Christ in ministry is often what causes us to stumble, as we wrestle with difficult issues like the authority of men in the church, our small paychecks, or the double standard of behavior that many of us experience.

After reading this chapter, I hope you will take some time to think and pray about your commitment to your fair treatment and how it impacts your faith response to God. Seeing its destructive power in our lives as we continuously bump up against the unfairness of life in ministry may surprise us. I must admit that I have wasted much prayer time arguing with God about the unfair way I am treated. I sit in judgment on his unwillingness to do things my way. I pout and complain. The fruit and gifts of the Spirit will not flourish in a heart filled with resentment and bitterness. There is no more fertile ground for resentment and bitterness to grow than when I judge God's care by my expectation of fair treatment.

Let's think for a moment about the idea of *fair*. We have all heard people glibly say that if God were *fair*, we would be in trouble. Of course, that is true. We did not deserve to have Jesus die for us. It was fundamentally unfair for the perfect Son of God to pay for our sins. However, that's not what normally concerns us. The context in which we Christians normally think about fairness is in the present with regard to ourselves.

We assess our ability to keep God's commandments or pray regularly and then expect a certain response from God based on our efforts. If we are doing well, we expect God to welcome us because it is only fair that he would favor his obedient children. We compare ourselves to others to assure ourselves of his friendly welcome. If we haven't been doing so well in our efforts to obey, we shy away from him, assuming that he won't be interested in us until we have something to show for ourselves. Approaching God from this skewed perspective ensures that we will alternate between pride and despair. When we are committed to "all things fair," we can't help but experience God as judge, which causes us to hide, cover, and explain away our sin. When we forget what Jesus has done for us and instead rely on our own efforts to obey, we are stuck making our case for acceptance before him day after day.

Having said that, in one sense, it *is* completely fair that God would love us, favor us, welcome us into his presence, answer our prayers, and extend his faithfulness to us in every way. Think about what Jesus accomplished for us on the cross. There, God poured all of his wrath and judgment for our sin onto his Son. Although he was innocent, Christ endured God's anger to pay the penalty for our sin. For those who trust in Christ, there is no more payment to be made. There is no balance due. So the unjust suffering Jesus endured for our sake makes it fair for us to have a restored relationship with God—with all the benefits that accompany it. The penalty cannot be paid twice if God is to remain just. Since I am now perfectly righteous in Christ, I am perfectly deserving of being God's child and a part of his family. God was perfectly righteous to adopt me and make me his own. Because of the cross, I am no waif but a perfect daughter in whom he delights. The scope of what Christ did for us on the cross is almost unbelievable. He gave us perfect standing before the Holy God.

Even so, we sinners are prone to take ownership of what belongs to God and twist it so that it belongs to us. With the idea of fair, we view ourselves as fair-minded and reasonable and God as unfair and intractable. This is often a non-Christian's reason for not believing in God. After a natural disaster, an untimely death, or an injustice, God's fairness is questioned. Even as his children, we judge him for not acting fairly if he does not respond or behave in ways we think are right.

Many times I have judged God by what I felt was his unfair treatment of me. This is a recurring theme in my life. Recently, after fifteen months of support raising and living out of a suitcase, Josiah and I began the process of relocating to Philadelphia for our work with Serge. We checked into a moderate hotel and contacted a realtor to begin our house search. The search did not go as I had expected and weeks passed. One-room living at the Day's Inn was taking its toll. It seemed only reasonable to expect God to provide a house sooner rather than later. We were tired from our time of living out of suitcases. We had two extended overseas trips on the calendar, and opportunities for house hunting were limited to several three-week periods between those long trips. Sometimes I would take my computer and sit in my car in the hotel parking lot just to be alone so that I could think and write. After many disappointing days of house hunting I realized that I had expected God to provide quickly the house that we needed. We were working hard in trying circumstances. Why did God wait so long to provide a more permanent place for us to live?

What funny ways we bargain and negotiate with God! We have such fixed expectations about how life should go that we often miss the *quid pro quo* attitudes we have toward God. When we feel that God has not lived up to his part of the bargain, we criticize and judge his actions. We complain and grumble. We question his fairness. When we were outbid on the first house we pursued which I felt was *the one,* I was completely discouraged. A few days after we were outbid, we hopped on a plane to Africa. Wasn't God paying attention to our difficulties? Why didn't he give us that house? We may choke on the suggestion that we sit in judgment of God, but we often do just that.

When we criticize and complain about God's actions, we are judging him. Our finite human viewpoint, however, puts us at a definite disadvantage. We are not omniscient. We do not have all the pieces to the puzzle. Our analysis of fairness is always comparative and biased by our limitations. Our humanity creates a weakness that only faith can overcome. When we judge what God is doing by what we can see rather than by what he has said, we easily come to an unrighteous conclusion: God is not good. He doesn't care. God is not pleased with me. He isn't acting fairly. God must not love me. We are convinced we know best and accuse God of being unfair because he isn't doing what we want him to do. The daily battle for believers is to believe Scripture even when it conflicts with our expectations. The battle is lost when we draw insidious conclusions about God because of our biases and limited perspective. The resulting resentment and bitterness may seem directed at others but in truth they are directed toward God who, we believe, has somehow let us down and acted unfairly.

I once knew a talented woman who worked in a stateside discipleship ministry. She had worked in the organization for a number of years when I met her. As many of her colleagues married, her faith began to waver. Although other women in the organization were unmarried and seemingly content, she really wanted to be married. Those who lived with her felt her frustration, which resulted in bursts of irritation and rule-making for those around her. She was clearly disappointed with God, who was not bringing the husband she had anticipated as she devoted herself to ministry. She struggled with bitterness and an uncertainty of God's love because he had let her down and not answered her prayers for the married life she so desperately wanted. Why was God so unfair? Others had found husbands—why hadn't she? I think we have all been like my friend, with high expectations of how and when God should answer our prayers.

When we are not given the fair treatment we think we deserve, the resulting fruit is evident: resentment, bitterness, anger, joylessness, frustration, sleepless nights, manipulation, lack of love, and judgmental attitudes—the antithesis of the fruit of the Spirit. When we are committed to what *we* think is right, to *our* notion of fair, we are subject to the new laws of fairness that we have created. Galatians 5:18 says, "But if you are led by the Spirit, you are not under the law," yet we continue to put ourselves—and others, including God—under laws of our own making (like our standards for fairness), laws we cannot keep yet use to judge others and God. We choose this yoke of slavery over freedom in Christ and in so doing abandon the power and joy of being led by the Spirit. We have all experienced the misery that comes when we hang on to our right to fairness.

During a missions weekend at a large stateside church, I was approached by one of the assistant pastors' wives. As we talked, she began to lament the position she was in. She had just finished cleaning the kitchen after a dessert social. She was visibly exhausted. As her small children ran circles around us, she complained of the high expectations placed on her and her family by church members. She also complained about being denied the free vacations, free childcare, dinner invitations, and general respect and help that were offered to the senior pastor. She was unable to get past the unfair treatment she and her family had received. She was jealous and angry, on the verge of giving up and in no mood to talk about Jesus.

I was not around long enough to see how God interrupted this woman's tangle of unbelief, but I know that he faithfully pursues us even in our grumbling. It's the only hope we have. Christ desires us to enjoy the freedom he purchased for us on the cross, so he continually disrupts our bad theology and demands for fair treatment, often with something as mundane as a sink full of dishes.

Christ also interrupts our wrong thinking by pointing us to the law. Jesus summed it up this way: We are to love God with all of our being and love our neighbors in the same way we love ourselves (Matthew 22:37–40). Christ's summation of the law is a litmus test that reveals what is going on inside us. Loving God and loving others are fruits of his Spirit, tangible results of our inner faith connection, moment by moment, to Christ's work for us. When the fruit of love is replaced by our sinful response to God and to others, we can be sure we have somehow returned to our own efforts at law keeping. We cannot keep Christ's law of love without the Spirit's work in us. Our failure to do so indicates that our faith has shifted from Christ back to ourselves. Ministry introduces a profusion of people into our lives who expose our failure to love. Beyond family and friends, roommates and coworkers, we fill our lives with relationships that give us opportunities to speak about Christ. To expect fair treatment from all of these people is unrealistic. The power to love those who may not share our interests and values or who treat us badly is only possible as a fruit of the Spirit.

Difficult people reveal the true quality of our love. Its shallowness is exposed by our response to those who nitpick, criticize, have an agenda, don't appreciate us, cause us extra work, and oppose us. There are difficult people on our mission teams and in our churches, Bible study groups, and sometimes even in our homes. Our commitment to our notion of fairness is revealed when we complain to God about having to love them. Our commitment to our view of fairness is exposed when we excuse our failures to love by reminding God that we love *most* of the people we know. We think this should be good enough for God. We make excuses regarding those we avoid and ignore because we find them demanding, offensive, and impossible to love. We may even blame God for bringing so many challenging people our way! Jesus's interruptions into our lives are extremely inconvenient as he brings us people who are difficult to like, much less love and serve. His law of love exposes the depth and breadth of our need for him each day.

We often behave like ungrateful and petty children, but our Father loves us and does not give up on us. With love and tenderness, he disciplines us by introducing difficulty into our lives. He exposes our general self-orientation and commitment to our fair treatment. With each difficulty he introduces into our day, he gives us a choice. We can respond with a suspicious, judging, and unbelieving heart (What is God doing now?), or we can take our confusion and questions to him, believing that he loves us and has our best interests at heart, believing that his actions are always righteous and true.

I don't know why God took so long to supply a house for us, but every day I had a choice. I could trust that he was caring for us in our temporary situation (which included a family of mice) and be thankful for a bed to sleep in or I could grumpily remind him that we were working for him as I complained about our accommodations. These were decisions I had to revisit whenever worry, doubt, and frustration intruded and I felt God had treated us unfairly. God will continue to bring difficult situations and people into your life and mine to show us where we have forgotten his love. It's important to him that we remember it.

There are definitely challenges in the realities most of us are up against. If you are single, you may be trying to figure out how to meet potential marriage partners. You may be navigating a series of ever-changing roommates, never feeling settled in your life, or struggling with chronic loneliness. If you are married to someone who questions his gifts or calling, you will be deeply affected. If your husband is always "right" and questions your actions instead of his own, you will feel alone and unsupported. If your marriage has grown cold and you feel unloved, you will have many challenges. Do you have rebellious kids or children with special needs? Does someone in your family have serious health issues? Many people in ministry have had a brush with depression. We're all tempted to wonder about the fairness of our lives at times. If we are to believe that Jesus came to heal the sick and that he is smart enough to know our life situations, then we have to believe that he knew who we were when he called us into ministry. Faith believes he can work *in* us at the same time he is working *through* us. That is our only hope in ministry.

Christian ministry is a hard place to have problems, but the solution is always the same. The gospel speaks to each of us where we are. There are no lost causes or hopeless cases with Christ. Some of us may have health issues that need to be addressed to relieve our difficulties. Others of us may need to work through life issues with a counselor. All of us will benefit from the encouragement we receive from friendships, books, and other resources, but no amount of human help will fill our emptiness if it does not lead us *to* Christ. His is the voice we need to hear. Sometimes we just need help to be able to hear it.

Years ago I met a young missionary at a renewal conference. As we met together, she told me the story of her life and the abuse she had suffered as a child. She had been meeting with a counselor and had faced what had been done to her, and a deep healing process was well underway in her heart. But she admitted that she still did not feel the closeness to Christ that she desired. She had made great steps in forgiving her abuser. She was functioning well on her mission team and was excited about the work she was doing. Still, she felt disconnected from Christ.

As we began to talk, it was evident that she had little sense of her own need for a Savior. She knew what it meant to need rescue from the sins of others, but could not connect with the idea that she also needed rescue from her own sins. She believed theologically that she was a sinner, but could only think of tiny examples of sin. As we began to speak about God's love for her and the work Christ had accomplished for her on the cross, she began to realize that many of her efforts in life had been to prove that she was a good person who deserved love. Love had never been offered to her as a gift, and she was having a hard time accepting God's free gift of love, forgiveness, and righteousness. The idea that freely admitting her sin would bring her closer to Christ was a new one. By the end of the week she left with a few ideas of her real need for a Savior and a new realization that she no longer had to prove her worth to God. Because of Jesus she was worthy of God's love and accepted into his family and even though she was still broken, she responded with gratitude and hope.

The world is a mess. We are a mess. The gospel is not a sidebar to real life, but the source of all real life for us. Ministry jades us. It exposes us to bad stuff. We all experience the fallout. Bob Dylan expresses the mess well in "Everything Is Broken."[6] With his usual insightfulness, he expresses the brokenness of our lives in everything from our possessions to our relationships. The refrain pushes us to stop kidding ourselves; everything in this world is broken.

This would be a great song to play before the Sunday sermon. If we could get into our heads just how broken we are—our families, our churches, our cities, our world—then all of us would be ready to hear the gospel as good news. Everything *is* broken. Every unbeliever who walks through the door of the church knows it. The person we talk to in the coffee shop knows it. So does the woman in the unemployment line. What makes church feel artificial to those unfamiliar with its culture is that, even though we say Jesus died for broken sinners in a broken world, we work to keep those sinners out of our churches and out of our lives. Their needs are messy, expensive, and time-consuming. When we are blind to our own brokenness and need for a Savior, our talk of *good news* will be hollow. But when we clearly understand that everything is broken, our offer of a Savior who has overcome the brokenness will ring true to unbelievers and to us. We are not offering organized religion or good works, law-keeping or principles for living, but a Savior for our broken lives and our broken world.

We need strength to be honest about ourselves without getting bogged down in our sin. We are sinners, yet in the kingdom of God we are welcome. When we see Jesus, we don't wallow in the muck of our sinfulness or the brokenness of our lives or our world; we go to meet him. He gives us joy even in hard times. When we are with him, we can finally forget ourselves, brokenness and all, and be truly free. Is everything broken? Yes, but Jesus has taken care of that. The cross was the ultimate place of brokenness. There the Son of God was broken for our sin. By his stripes we are healed. The good news is truly good; we now belong to him. So let's repent and stop griping about what is not fair. Nothing much is fair! Life will not be fixed until Jesus returns. We can work for healing and social justice, but we can't create a kingdom of fairness in which to live. Our calling is to offer the gospel of Christ as God's solution to a broken and unfair world.

There have been many times when I have suddenly realized how hard my heart had grown toward God. As often as not, it had to do with something I thought wasn't fair. It's easy to look at others in ministry who seem to have it better than we do (be it family, money, marriages, talents, donors, houses, churches, or whatever) and think that God has been unfair to us. It would be inappropriate to cite the situations and people I have complained about to God over the years, but the list is extensive! I easily forget how broken I am. But there is no sense in kidding myself, I need Jesus every day and so do you.

We are not hopeless or in despair like those without Christ. We have the hope of redemption for ourselves and for the world. Paul encourages Timothy the church planter this way: "You then, my child, be strengthened by the grace that is in Christ Jesus" (2 Timothy 2:1). We need to be strengthened by the grace we find in Christ. His grace keeps us from running away from the brokenness we encounter or from being overwhelmed by it. His grace strengthens our faith so that we can believe that we are accepted by God and encourage others in their believing. His grace brings hope. His grace opens us to the love of God. The grace of Christ brings with it the full weight of all he has done for us. The despair that brokenness brings loses its power when we stand in the grace of Christ.

We no longer find our identity in our brokenness, but rather in our redemption. Filled with the grace of Christ, we are able to believe God's promises to us. Now we are strong enough to offer Christ to others in their brokenness.

Sometimes ministry women huddle in a little Christian cocoon, lacking the inner strength to deal with the reality around us. This is why our presentation of the gospel makes no sense to others—because it really makes no sense to us. If we are not strengthened by the grace of Christ for the sin and brokenness that remain in us, we will have nothing to offer others. We need to stop hiding from our brokenness as if our hiding will keep us safe. Jesus is with us. *He* will keep us safe. The gospel jars us into the broken reality of our lives and our world and it is here that ministry happens. Our struggles with issues like fairness evaporate when we awaken to the truth of the gospel. Jesus was broken for the sins of the world; he was broken for us. "With his wounds we are healed" (Isaiah 53:5). This is the gospel of hope we believe for ourselves and offer to others.

What Are Your Thoughts?

1. Think of injustices you have experienced. How did these injustices affect your prayer life?

2. What do you complain about to God?

3. Is your heart strong enough to engage the brokenness of this world or do you keep yourself sheltered? How has this affected your ability to understand the gospel for yourself and explain the gospel to unbelievers?

4. Do you believe that Jesus understands and sympathizes with your struggles?

5. Think of an area of your life where you struggle to trust Christ because you do not understand or like what he is doing. Are you willing to bring your arguments to Christ and allow him to change your mind?

Pause and Reset
Grace to Help

Since then we have a great high priest who has passed
through the heavens, Jesus, the Son of God, let us hold
fast our confession. For we do not have a high priest
who is unable to sympathize with our weaknesses, but
one who in every respect has been tempted as we are, yet
without sin. Let us then with confidence draw near to the
throne of grace, that we may receive mercy and find grace
to help in time of need. (Hebrews 4:14–16)

I cannot think of anyone with more reason than Jesus to feel
that his life experiences were unfair. His Father asked him to put
off his eternal heavenly form to put on human flesh that he would
then wear forever. He left an eternity of worship and adoration to
become a person without standing, wealth, or power. He never
sinned, but was constantly surrounded by sinners who misunderstood and abused him. Everything about his life circumstances was
humbling, from his education to his hometown. The Holy Son of
God never received preferential treatment or a kingly welcome.

What was life like for the perfect Son of God? He grew up in the
home of a carpenter with brothers and sisters. He was the Word by
whom the world was created, yet his education consisted of Torah
and vocational training. When we hear the commandment to
honor your father and your mother, we realize that Jesus honored
Mary and Joseph perfectly. Having been both a child and a par-
ent, I find it difficult to imagine obeying just this one commandment. I remember how unreasonable I thought my parents were at
times, and I know how hard it has been for my children to honor
their imperfect mom. The one story we have from Jesus's childhood
is his visit to the temple as a twelve-year-old (Luke 2:41–52). He
stayed behind to listen to the teachers and to ask them questions.

They were amazed at his understanding and his answers, yet life was already mapped out for him. He was to apprentice as a carpenter. The passage states that he was submissive to his parents; he lived an obscure life as a carpenter until he was about thirty years old and his public ministry began.

As we think about who Jesus is and what life was like for him, this passage takes on great weight. Jesus was tempted in *every way* that we are and yet he did not sin. The number of opportunities he must have had to think, "This is not fair; I do not deserve this," is incalculable. Yet we know he never gave in to temptation because God accepted him as the perfect sacrifice for our sin. There was no blemish in him. Jesus knows the weight and power of our temptations because he was one of us. He knows that our sin nature makes us vulnerable to temptation, which is one reason he is so full of sympathy toward us. He has felt the pressure of our temptations, even as the sinless Son of God.

I have had many conversations with pastors' wives who wrestle with the unfair way they and their husbands have been treated. Many of us have been in a congregational meeting where our husbands were cruelly criticized and yet we were expected to leave the meeting with a smile on our face and no ill will. Pastor's wives are often expected to have no real feelings, as if we are robots instead of women. When people stand up in public and say bad things about our husbands, we struggle with the unfairness of it all because we know about the long hours and sacrifices they have made. The church is full of believing and unbelieving sinners—emphasis on the word *sinners*. Missionaries often wrestle with the unfair distribution of wealth in the church as we return home. We have seen the poverty of the church in many parts of the world and the dwindling balance of our own support accounts. We often find the paternalistic answers and selfishness of the American church frustrating as our pleas for help are minimized or ignored. We will be treated unfairly at times. We will get angry at times. People will make us cry at times. And yes, at times we will be discouraged by the whole mess and ready to give up.

The place we go for help and comfort is not described as a throne of power, but as a throne of grace. Unlike the response we sometimes receive from the sinners we serve, the reception we will find when we come to Christ with our hurts and frustrations will always be a gracious one. He has done everything required to give us the confidence we need to come boldly to him. As we pour out our hearts to him he comforts us; he understands. Since we are never without sin in those difficult situations, he is tenderhearted in his offer of mercy because he knows that our hearts will waver when our sin is revealed. We will need that mercy, as we own our sin when others do not. Then he fills us with his Spirit and sends us out with his gracious power strengthening us in every way. Our repentance and faith make us tender toward God and toward others. Our hard edges demand to be treated fairly and can only be softened in Christ's presence. As we receive his grace time and time again, it will work deep change in us.

When our right to fair treatment begins to permeate our attitudes and opinions, an alarm should go off inside our heads, warning us that our expectations have disconnected us from Christ's presence and love. As the Spirit awakens us to our condition, we know where to go for help. Jesus has already provided the sacrifice for our sins. He wants us to experience his mercy so that he can fill us with the grace we need to say no to our selfish expectations and the unrealistic expectations of those around us. His grace comforts us and makes us brave enough to step into a world of sinners, even as broken sinners ourselves.

> For consider your calling, [sisters]: not many of you were
> wise according to worldly standards, not many were
> powerful, not many were of noble birth. But God chose
> what is foolish in the world to shame the wise; God chose

what is weak in the world to shame the strong; God chose what is low and despised in the world, even things that are not, to bring to nothing things that are, so that no human being might boast in the presence of God. And because of him you are in Christ Jesus, who became to us wisdom from God, righteousness and sanctification and redemption, so that, as it is written, "Let the one who boasts, boast in the Lord." (1 Corinthians 1:26–31)

If we think of things from God's perspective, it does not seem *fair* that we would be the messengers he chooses to spread his good news. We can be a sorry lot at times, yet God has chosen us to represent him in this world. He has always favored the weak and the foolish to be his voice. After the resurrection of Christ, the spread of the gospel through the ministry of the apostles was absolutely amazing. Much of the doubt about Christianity and the veracity of Scripture come from a natural incredulity that so much could spring from so little.

God's way of doing things in this world is ever surprising. I find it amazing that he has used me over the years. I am not confused about the smallness of my life or the bigness of this world. You may need to take a fresh look at yourself and marvel at the things God has done through you. When we are honest about our brokenness and God's amazing answer to the troubles of this world, the glory of Christ is revealed in us and no one will doubt who is to be thanked and praised, worshiped and honored.

Chapter 8

The Pit of Entitlement and Envy

Pit: a hole in the ground.
Entitlement: the right to have something.
Envy: resentful desire of something possessed by another.
(Wiktionary)

THERE IS AN old song by Cab Calloway entitled, "A Chicken Ain't Nothin' but a Bird."[7] I love his big band sound and pithy lyrics, which are energizing and fun to sing when it's time to clean the house. But what I particularly like about this song is its apt description of a common human frailty to assign fancy names to plain old stuff. What's more, we are unfailingly eager to shade the truth about ourselves to ensure that we are seen in a good light. For example, we often refer to our anger as frustration and our gossip as concern. We rename our sin and speak half-truths about ourselves to appear better than we are.

When we examine ourselves for traces of envy and entitlement, what we discover may unsettle us. As we confront the crushing thought that we might have a problem with entitlement and the envy that drives it, we are tempted to find a fancy way to describe these old birds. Entitlement becomes "something we deserve"; our envy is the cynical response we have to an unfair world. These evasive strategies come naturally to us, but, as believers, our lives take on a fictitious quality if we cannot call our sin by its real name, even sins as hard to own as entitlement and envy. Regardless of how well our "chicken" is dressed, it is still true that "a chicken ain't nothin' but a bird."

Ministry is hard. The only people who fully appreciate its rigors are those who are in it. It's only natural to pity ourselves in our struggles. We give in to self-indulgence to cope with the pressures we face. We fall into self-pity as we compare our difficulties to those whose lives appear worry-free. We question God's goodness and, before you know it, we find ourselves in a smelly cesspool where entitlement, envy, and other emotional dreck collect and flourish. It's a scary place, yet I think we have all been there.

With every thought of entitlement we nurture, we fall deeper into the pit. Whether we deserve a bigger house for ministry, an SUV for transport, a husband more sensitive to our needs, or recognition for our sacrifices, we feel entitled because we give so much to others. Our belief that we deserve a little extra for our service opens the door to envy. Have you ever envied someone with a large house who rarely entertains? How about the woman with a large vehicle whose children are grown? Do you envy women whose husbands bring them flowers or plan getaway weekends? How do you feel when someone's work is recognized and yours goes unnoticed? When your friend finds a husband and you don't? Every envious response that comes from our sense of entitlement mires us more deeply in our dishonesty. We believe our own spin: *I deserve more.*

The hardships of ministry expose the dark places of our hearts where the gospel has not yet penetrated. The Holy Spirit often uses life's everyday occurrences to illuminate the dark corners where our sins lurk. As he reveals sins like entitlement and envy, it's easy for us to despair or run away from the dark rebellion he has exposed.

Hearing the truth about our sin is painful, but Jesus comes and binds our wounds with his forgiveness, bringing us hope that he can change us in ways that seem impossible in the chaos of ministry.

A number of years ago after returning to the States from living overseas, I began to notice that my spiritual life was flat. Life had not turned out the way I expected and I was feeling sorry for myself. My precious grandchildren lived on the West Coast and I on the East. All three of my adult children were busy with their own lives and scattered, so I saw them only a few times a year. Then I had one of those weeks where everywhere I went I saw grandmothers and their grandkids. It was the perfect storm of self-indulging self-pity as I looked with envy at those grandmothers. They were so ordinary and I was so special! Why did they get to be with their grandchildren? What made them so deserving? Wasn't I entitled to the same happiness?

Like most grandparents, I have a great time with my grandkids. When I visit they hop into bed with me in the mornings and we watch Gran's latest YouTube finds or read a story. I love hearing their voices. I love when they lay their hand on my arm. I love the simple sincerity in their faces when they ask for something. I love snuggling in a chair to read a book. I love being on the floor with them and making up games to play and decoding Lego directions. I particularly love the precious conversations we have in the moment. None of these translate well to Skype or FaceTime. With each visit I gather bits and pieces of understanding about them so that I can come away feeling that I know them. But regardless of my efforts, my limited experiences only give me snapshots of who they are. I won't know them nor will they know me in that everyday way that comes from just being together.

This loss of relationship is hard for me, but I am only one of many who live at a distance from their families. In fact Josiah and I had taken our children away from *their* grandparents when we pursued church planting and then overseas missions. So why should

I write about how much I miss my grandkids? Because the Spirit used these particular struggles to show me that I had a serious problem with entitlement and envy.

In my third year as a grandmother, when tasks and events were piling up at Christmas, I wandered into our home library looking for something to read. (Reading is my preferred method of procrastination.) In my search I came across a small green book appropriately entitled *Envy*.[8]

Just reading the title made my heart sink. The Holy Spirit was speaking to me.

As jarring as such moments are for us, they are highly desirable in the life of a believer. When God gets our attention in such a pointed way, it usually indicates that he is about to do a significant work in us. It's true that he frequently works without our knowing, but in these encounters he invites us into the process to build our faith and strengthen our relationship with him.

Pretty sure that this was going to be one of those times, I decided that the little green book would stay on the shelf until the holidays were over. The celebration of Christ's incarnation would have been a perfect time to invite the Spirit to do his work, but I was hosting several Christmas parties and had family coming to stay; I knew how much physical and emotional energy this would require. Adding to my holiday to-do list "examining yourself for deep sin patterns you have been blind to" felt a bit over the top. So I intentionally avoided reading *Envy* that day. Nevertheless, in his gentle way, the Spirit began to give me a preview of what was to come.

The idea of envy began to churn away in my brain, and snippets of envious moments began to surface unbidden into my thought life. Just that Sunday, I'd had a conversation about grandchildren with a woman at our church. As her grandchildren ran circles around her, she commented that she would never be able to live at distance from them. I don't think she intended to imply that I was a heartless troll who had chosen to live far from my grandkids, but that's how I felt. I left depressed and envious. As I remembered this encounter, I began to suspect that the bad news about my envy was truly bad. I began to ask God to prepare me to receive this bad news and strengthen me to embrace the good news I would need to hear.

When the holidays were over and everyone had gone home, I returned to our library. Apparently, no one else in the family had felt the need to read about envy because the book was where I had left it. Pulling that little green volume from the shelf with a mixture of hope and dread, I began to read. I was certain that the Spirit would speak to me through it; and as I read, thought, and prayed, I felt as if I were standing at the edge of an abyss. What began to surface from its depths was surprising to me. It was malice.

I had never thought myself guilty of malice, but as I read about envy I began to understand that envy is malice toward another. The Spirit would not let me minimize this. Over the next few weeks, I started to see how envy had intruded into my life through seemingly innocent desires like being near my grandkids. I realized that the source of much of my envy was a deep sense of entitlement I had never seen. Entitlement takes root when we feel we deserve something. Because I wanted it so much, I had begun to act as if living near my grandchildren was something I deserved.

But our God is faithful. He didn't allow me to continue on this destructive path for long. Post-holiday laundry and cleaning were a cinch compared with the work of believing that, despite all of the ugliness that was revealed in me, I had not lost my place in God's family. I was welcomed as righteous and free from his judgment because of the cleansing blood of Christ.

If you think of yourself as a nice person being guilty of envy is especially embarrassing. Nothing about it evokes a smidgen of sympathy or compassion from anyone. It reveals inner darkness. Envy implies malice, which is aggressively evil. It requires harm to another for its satisfaction. Envy only wins when another loses.

When I began to see and then to say that I had a problem with envy and the entitlement that drives it, friends did not know what to say to me. It made for some very awkward conversations. They had thought I was such a nice spiritual person, and now I was giving them evidence to the contrary. My sin made them uncomfortable and humbled me.

Our days aren't usually filled with seeing such pervasive sin; if they were, we would never get out of bed. Normally we see our need for Christ in bits and pieces, growing and making progress in tiny increments. Nevertheless, when we are stuck and can't move forward or when we are on the cusp of ministry that will require an extra measure of faith, Jesus comes to us and opens a room in our interior lives that needs some light.

These times of disclosure are difficult, but they can work lasting fruit in us. Our faith revives, our trust in Christ's love is renewed and strengthened, our attachment to this world is diminished, our love for others is more genuine and less selfish, and we have a more realistic view of the cost of our sin. Thankfulness becomes the cadence of our hearts. As we bring our tangled web of sin to Jesus, he does not flinch but welcomes us into his presence and comforts us with his mercy. Seeing the sin that remains in us reveals our present need of his cleansing blood and reminds us of the provision he has already made for us.

The Bible talks a lot about humility. Being humble is a healthy element in our spiritual lives. Yet we cannot become humble by our own efforts. God must work humility in us and he frequently does so by showing us our sin. It is embarrassing to be humbled in this way. Our concern for our reputation pushes us to avoid the moment as long as possible. Yet when God reveals our inability to say no to sin, even after all he has done for us, our pride is interrupted. Paul describes our predicament well: "I have the desire to do what is right, but not the ability to carry it out. For I do not do the good I want, but the evil I do not want is what I keep on doing"

(Romans 7:18b–19). Not only do we frequently give in to temptation and sin, we botch our most sincere efforts to do good which humbles us at the most basic level.

As we step into the light of Christ's presence, more of our sin is revealed. It is an irony of the Christian life. If we want to be with Jesus, we must be prepared for the light of his presence to reveal the sin that remains in us. Near the end of his life, when Paul describes himself as the "foremost" of sinners (1 Timothy 1:15b), we realize that he must have spent much time in God's presence to have this opinion of himself. Many of us who are long-time believers share Paul's experience. The more we come to know Christ, the more we need him. I shared my struggle with entitlement and envy with several women who, I'm afraid, never quite recovered their good opinion of me. There are those who cannot help but put us on a spiritual pedestal, and if we are open about the work Christ is doing in us, sooner or later our lives will disappoint them.

Daily admission of sin and our need for Christ is humbling, but the nature of the humility he works in us is not what we might expect. Christ does not seek to put us in our place, but rather to reorient us to the reality of who he is and what he has done for us. "[Jesus], being in very nature God, did not consider equality with God something to be used to his own advantage; rather, he made himself nothing by taking the very nature of a servant, being made in human likeness. And being found in appearance as a man, he humbled himself by becoming obedient to death—even death on a cross! Therefore God exalted him to the highest place" (Philippians 2:6–9a NIV). We grow in humility as we come to know this Christ who died for sinners. We are humbled because our sin caused his suffering and pain. The cost of our sin becomes real to us when the Spirit reveals the specifics of the sin for which Jesus died. As our sin is revealed and we agree that we need the cleansing blood of Christ yet again, our belief opens us to the work of the Spirit who produces fruit from our repentance.

131

Being graciously received when we bring our sin to Christ strengthens our faith in the efficacy of the cross. We experience its powerful effects each time God welcomes us; we trust more deeply each time he responds with mercy and grace. As we experience his gracious welcome, we can hear Christ's words to us without fear: "Those whom I love, I reprove and discipline, so be zealous and repent. Behold, I stand at the door and knock. If anyone hears my voice and opens the door, I will come in to him and eat with him, and he with me" (Revelation 3:19–20).

The Spirit's work to show us our sin and need for Christ is born out of love. He urges us to be zealous when our sin is revealed. In the vernacular, the Spirit urges us to hard-core repenting. He wants us to get busy so that when Christ knocks, we will be quick to open our doors to him instead of hiding in the closet. Jesus knocks on our doors because he desires to come in and sit with us for a meal— a most friendly, intimate, and satisfying encounter. Jesus offers us himself—he wants a relationship with us. He becomes real beyond our theology. We begin the lifelong adventure of getting to know him and having many such meals with him. We rely on Jesus to be the bread (John 6:35) that sustains us. He paid for our sins and brought us into his family. He prepared the way for us to know him intimately and to belong to him. When he enters our hearts, he does not cease to be the Holy Eternal God, but we may receive him without fear because of what he has done for us. He is our place of safety and from this safe place we can hear what he has to say to us without worry.

Living in God's presence reveals the bottomless well of sin in us. After all Christ has done, after all his love and care, we still seek other sources for the bread we need. We forget who we are. We wander and we sin. Our lives resemble an arcade game where an oversized hammer is used to whack critters that continually pop up through too many holes. Every kind of sin continues to pop up in our lives, regardless of how big our hammers and how diligently we whack. We will never stop needing Christ's blood to cover our sin or his Physician's touch to heal our wounds. Sin will continue to pop up in our lives and humble us.

As humbled sinners, we learn not to trust our efforts to reform ourselves, but to trust only in Christ's work to make us clean. When Paul refers to himself as "foremost sinner," he ranks himself at the top of the list of those who need the cleansing blood of Christ. His cry resonates deeply in those of us who have seen the dark places of our hearts and we can only imagine what Paul must have seen in his. But Jesus offers himself to the repentant sinner. That is his message to first-time repenters and to those who have come to him many times. As he sits down with us for a meal, we realize that he is the Bread we have been craving. I am grateful that Jesus continues to knock on my door and provide bread for my hungry heart. We can trust him. He is faithful and will never stop knocking, even when we are slow to answer. Looking at our sin is challenging, but repentance is the door through which Christ will enter our lives to have fellowship with us. "So sinful, so weary, Thine, Thine would I be; Thou blest Rock of Ages, I'm hiding in Thee."[9]

So, what was my response when the Spirit showed me the effect that entitlement and envy had on my life? I felt truly sad for the love I had withheld from God and from others to hang onto it. And my love for Jesus grew deeper as I experienced his forgiveness and mercy for even these sins. I saw the Holy Spirit begin to work real change in me. I often find myself minimizing or ignoring the Spirit's convicting voice, but this time God revealed the ugliness of my sin in a way I could not ignore. I didn't have a shred of hope that I could fix it. There was nothing to do but agree with him.

Seeing the ugliness inside of me was painful, but God's desire was to show me this awful area of sin so that I could be free of it. He wanted to make me aware of its poisonous influence on my life and allow me to work with him to make real progress. This is often the way the Spirit works. He reveals sin and then unfolds his plan to change us. As we repent of the sin he shows us and believe in the power of the cross for that particular sin, we move from faith to faith. We believe God is working because we *see* him working. We grow in our willingness to trust in his love and care, even when he reveals the darkness in our hearts.

What Are Your Thoughts?

1. Name something you think God owes you.

2. Is there anyone you envy? What do they have that you want?

3. How has God humbled you recently?

4. Do you find it hard to believe that God loves you? Why or why not?

5. Do you feel safe as you read Christ's words in Revelation 3:19–20, or are "reprove" and "discipline" words that do not connote grace to you?

Pause and Reset
God Is for Us

What then shall we say to these things? If God is for us, who can be against us? He who did not spare his own Son but gave him up for us all, how will he not also with him graciously give us all things? Who shall bring any charge against God's elect? It is God who justifies. Who is to condemn? Christ Jesus is the one who died—more than that, who was raised—who is at the right hand of God, who indeed is interceding for us. Who shall separate us from the love of Christ? Shall tribulation, or distress, or persecution, or famine, or nakedness, or danger, or sword? As it is written, "For your sake we are being killed all the day long; we are regarded as sheep to be slaughtered." No, in all these things we are more than conquerors through him who loved us. For I am sure that neither death nor life, nor angels nor rulers, nor things present nor things to come, nor powers, nor height nor depth, nor anything else in all creation, will be able to separate us from the love of God in Christ Jesus our Lord. (Romans 8:31–39)

Women in ministry have faith that God will keep his promises, answer prayers, and move his kingdom forward through us. As we step out in faith, we trust God to meet us. Having expectations of God is not wrong. The work of the Spirit is to turn our attention expectantly toward God. What gets us into trouble is the content of our expectations. We give in to the notion that the sacrifices we have made for the gospel entitle us to special treatment.

When we were raising support for our first term in missions, some dear Christian friends gave us an old Chevy van to use for our travels. Aside from needing a paint job, the van had a unique feature: it had a side door platform fitted for a wheelchair. It is not difficult to imagine how our three teens felt about that van. Everywhere we went, we had to find two parking places so that the kids could exit the van via the elevator platform. (The van's configuration did not allow them to exit through the front doors.) Many a time our teens would have to follow after the van on foot as Dad circled a parking lot looking for a space big enough to allow them to climb back in, because another car had parked alongside us to block the side door entry. (Although we had a handicap van we did not have a handicap sticker!) After many months on the road, even the side door stopped latching and we had to use a rope to tie it closed. There was nothing cool about any of that.

My thankfulness for the van God had provided had been steadily waning, when en route to a mission conference in rural Mississippi, we had a flat tire. With a stony look, I said to my optimist husband, "Do not tell us what is good about this situation!" Of course, he could not resist and began to recount all the reasons why our situation could be worse. I, on the other hand, had expected a little special treatment from God for our willingness to take our teens on the road and then overseas. Surely we could be afforded a no-flat-tire status as we traveled to a mission conference! Our unbidden expectations that things go smoothly as we do God's work is a common hazard of ministry. The unspoken expectations we have of God only come to light when he graciously ignores them.

Why is entitlement a hazard of ministry? To *what* does ministry make us feel entitled? Embarking on ministry entails setting aside our plans and pursuit of happiness to serve others. Our focus might be students or the church, a foreign city or a small village. Who and where are up to God, but the nature of ministry is giving our lives for the lives of others.

I know many young women who have chosen to serve in remote areas of the world as teachers to missionary children. These women sacrifice building their careers and meeting potential mates to serve missionary families. Their importance to mission teams in isolated areas is often underestimated, but their work is crucial to the longevity of remote mission teams. These women give up the life they could have had at home to facilitate the work of the gospel in hard places.

What is the temptation for those us of who give up our lives for the gospel? We get into trouble when we believe that God owes us for our choice. We would never say this out loud. We are smart enough to remember Jesus's description of the workers who worked in a vineyard all day and complained when they received the same wage as those who came for the last hour (Matthew 20:1–16). Yet often we are those complaining workers who feel we deserve more than God has given. Our critique of the way God chooses to manage his vineyard creates a place in our hearts for a sense of entitlement to grow.

During our first Christmas in Ireland, we received a Christmas letter from a pastor's family we barely knew. We have all received these letters. Many of us write them. Each member of the family had a long paragraph written about their accomplishments for the year. The teenagers were excelling in a remarkable number of academic, sport, and social arenas. The parents' lives were full of their successes as parents, as people, and as Christian workers. It was hard to read about the blessings showered on this family as we struggled to integrate into Irish society. But the thing that tipped me over the edge that lonely Christmas was the last paragraph, which described the great year their family dog had. Did they seriously write an update on their *dog*?

We were so sad that Christmas. We missed home. Our lives had not yet been filled with the work, friends, and activities that give life meaning. Here was a letter describing a family that seemed to have everything (their dog had a better year than we did!) and we were feeling empty, lonely, and somewhat forgotten. Not only did I envy that family, but also if I had received a follow-up letter from them that highlighted losing teams, lousy SAT scores, a crabgrass infestation, and a mange epidemic, I would have felt a deep satisfaction about the disasters that had intruded into their perfect existence. That is malice! The saying "Misery loves company" endures for a reason. If I don't get what I want, I don't want anyone else to have it either. From the outside, God's care for that family and his care for our family were strikingly different. I thought I had counted the cost of taking our teens overseas, but seeing the contrast between our lives and the lives of this pastor's family revealed many hidden expectations I had about how God would manage the workers in his vineyard.

Where in our lives does entitlement thrive? If we take ourselves to Christ, he will show us what he wants us to see. I have had many expectations of God over the years. Here are just a few: marriage happiness (we are both Christians), successful ministry (we are much more dedicated than *those* guys), happy kids (we are serving you, Lord!), monetary security (why do the wicked prosper?), safety

(I'm your child, so bad things should not happen to me), beach vacations (I want it, I need it, I deserve it), no traffic jams today (I have important stuff to do), a better metabolism (all this traveling around is making me fat), access to my grandkids (the least you can do, God), freedom from health problems (people depend on me), not having to raise support for mission work (seriously?). I am constantly manufacturing an agenda for God to follow.

Although this is *my* abbreviated and unattractive list, perhaps it will prime the pump as you think about the agenda you have for God today. We are tempted to feel entitled in the big areas of life and in the mundane. No one is exempt. A missionary in the bush might resent that her housemate has the bigger bedroom. A suburban pastor's wife might feel she deserves the same educational options for her children as the folks in her church. It doesn't matter how little or how much we have—we always want just a little bit more. A result of the fall (Genesis 3) is that we relive Eve's moment over and over: "This fruit is just what I need." We are easily seduced into thinking we are entitled to it.

Romans 8:31–39 is Paul's answer to the hardships brought about by our sin and by life in ministry. The first thing Romans 8 accomplishes is to lift our eyes from ourselves to God. Yes, we have much remaining sin in our lives—ugly, destructive sins like entitlement, envy, and even malice. Yes, there are many confusing aspects to our lives that we wrestle to understand, but the meaning we long for is not found in ourselves or in our world. As believers, our lives are no longer measured by our law keeping. ("But now we are released from the law, having died to that which held us captive, so that we serve in the new way of the Spirit" [Romans 7:6].) Rather, our identity comes from our belonging to God. We are his children. Paul's answer to our struggle with remaining sin and the hardships of life is to stop looking within or at our circumstances. Paul tells us to look up.

The answer to Paul's rhetorical question of who can bring a charge against the elect is clear. If God has justified us, we are justified. No other charge can be brought against us. Even our own consciences have no right to condemn us. Jesus died for us and gave us perfect standing before God. He has pronounced us clean. Within the security of that relationship, we are able to look at the sin that remains in our lives. We can even look at the distressing, repetitive stuff. Taking our sin to the cross is the only way to be rid of it. Once we get over the shock of seeing our sin, we rejoice that we can again return to the cross. Christ's purpose is not to condemn, but to free us from the sin that weighs us down and trips us up. God is for us! The power of our flesh that just keeps on sinning, the press of a world resistant to the gospel, and the schemes of the Devil fade to nothing in light of this. Christ is interceding on our behalf. Who can stand against *him*?

Paul's list in verse 35—"tribulation, or distress, or persecution, or famine, or nakedness, or danger, or sword"—is particularly affecting to us who are in ministry. We have suffered some of the things Paul describes. Our suffering for the sake of the gospel is not theoretical. This passage describes *our* lives, at least to some extent, as we take the gospel to the world. Paul then asks a question that we ask ourselves when trouble comes. What dire circumstance will separate us from Christ's love? We often find ourselves in difficulties as we muck around in the lives of broken people and live in broken places. We could wrap ourselves in safety and ease, but we have chosen to put ourselves in situations that are beyond our control. We line up for the slaughter. The extreme events Paul describes in Romans 8 were from his own life. From tribulation to the sword, Paul describes his suffering to bring the gospel to the Gentiles. Yet through all he experienced, he was safe in Christ's love. In verse 35, Paul begins to build his argument. We will never be separated from Christ's love.

Where do you find yourself today? Unbelief can separate us from experiencing the love of Christ. His love for us is fixed and unwavering, but our experience can be changeable, so it is interesting that Paul begins with this list of extreme circumstances as he talks about the love of Christ. He clearly understands our frailty. For many of us, it does not take much to doubt God's love. If he says no to our prayers, we doubt his love. If our kids struggle, we doubt his love. If our bank account is low or ministry has not turned out as we planned, we doubt his love. If we are single and want to be married, we doubt his love. If we have a chronic illness or our relationships are troubled, we doubt his love. Many of us never get to the tribulation-distress-persecution-famine-nakedness-danger-sword part of ministry. We are like babies needing our milk of reassurance in the basics.

But Christ does not give up on us. He pushes and pulls us into his love. Much of the opposition and frustrations in our lives come from Christ pressing in on us. He wants us to know deep down in the secret places of our being, that he loves us. As we see the shallowness of our grasp of his love, we need not despair. We can go to him. We aren't doomed to uncertainty. He is eager to answer our cry to know his love. We can be the friend Jesus describes in Luke 11:5–8 and ask, seek, and knock on heaven's door until we get an answer. God wants us to know his love.

Some of us have a dim view of the transforming power of God's love, but I have seen that power in the lives of women in ministry. One woman was shy and never thought of herself as having anything to give. Yet as she began to grow in her experience of Christ's love, even though she did not feel confident of her Bible knowledge or have strong gifts of teaching, she began to lead a Bible study. The women in her area finally had someone they could relate to while hearing about Jesus. Why was this friend able to walk through her fear into the lives of these women? It was because she had begun to believe that God loved her, that he would answer her prayers for help, and that he would provide the competence she needed for ministry.

Another ministry wife was known for her great cooking but often used her skills to hide in the kitchen. Now, years later, you would not recognize the amazing gospel speaker she has become. When she began to discover anew what Jesus had done for her and how much he loved her, she had a story to tell. Her life of duty and obligation was replaced by the joy of talking of and living out a gospel that was real to her. These women were changed as they began to believe for themselves the ideas Paul expresses in Romans 8:31–34.

Knowing that God is for us breaks fear's hold over us and opens our hearts to his love. I saw his love change my friends so deeply that I hardly recognize them now. There is beauty and wisdom in the way Paul guides us through these ideas. God's gift of his Son convinces us of his great love for us. This love softens our hard hearts: "He who did not spare his own Son but gave him up for us all, how will he not also with him graciously give us all things?" (8:32). His love breaks the power of fear in our lives: "Who shall bring any charge against God's elect? . . . Who is to condemn?" (8:33–34). His love changes us: "Christ Jesus . . . who is at the right hand of God, who indeed is interceding for us" (8:34).

Paul, who has painstakingly laid out the mystery of the gospel in Romans 1–8, continues to speak of the power of Christ's love as he turns to the realm of the spiritual in verses 38–39. Life and death, angels and rulers, the present and the future, powers, anything below or anything above—nothing in all creation (which is everything other than God himself) can keep us from Christ's love. It would be amazing enough to survive all that Paul describes as possible scenarios for ministers of the gospel, but the power of Christ's love has an even more remarkable effect. We do not just survive ministry; we come through it triumphant, having conquered even the powerful foe of our unbelief. "We are more than conquerors through him who loved us" (8:37). Christ's love transforms us from those who shrink back from troubles to those who even in hardship find solace, rest, strength, and courage in his love. Paul spends so much time talking about Christ's love for us because he understands that it is both the motivation and the power we need to get up, leave our present struggles behind, and follow him today.

Chapter 9
Antacid of Choice

Antacid: an agent that counteracts or neutralizes acidity, especially in the stomach. (Wiktionary)

WALK INTO THE pharmacy and you will find a row of remedies for your acid woes   antacids. These magic potions are a product of our stressful world and I am grateful for them. I don't know anyone in ministry who, at the very least, doesn't have a roll of Tums handy when coffee and tense conversations collide. If our call is to love and care for people, it will surely include many stressful moments as we enter complicated lives to carry burdens and as we fight to avoid being overwhelmed by the weight of those burdens. Stress is not an evil to be avoided, although our health may suffer its effects, but a byproduct of ministry opportunities that come our way.

"For you know the grace of our Lord Jesus Christ, that though he was rich, yet for your sake he became poor, so that you by his poverty might become rich" (2 Corinthians 8:9). Christ has an unusual plan for making his work of redemption known; he gives his grace to unlikely people like us (1 Corinthians 1:26–29). By his grace we respond to his call and enter into the work with him. Only his grace changes us into those through whom his Spirit does extraordinary things. "And because of him you are in Christ Jesus, who became to us wisdom from God, righteousness and sanctification and redemption, so that, as it is written, 'Let the one who boasts, boast in the Lord'" (1 Corinthians 1:30–31).

We talk a lot about grace these days. I must confess that a number of years ago I got so sick of the word that I was determined to erase it from my vocabulary. It seemed to show up in every book, every song, and every new phrase, and its use became the new yardstick for spirituality. Of course, my response was silly and pointless, but we Western Christians have a nauseating ability to take something holy and good and market it as a commodity to spend on ourselves.

I think that, for many, God's grace has become a therapeutic resource to make us feel better about ourselves and about our choices, which then improves our spiritual standard of living. We may use our new freedom as an excuse to avoid commitment to a fellowship (our church planters really feel this one), give money sacrificially (our churches and our missionaries can testify here), study Scripture (young church planters and missionaries lack Bible knowledge that was considered basic in the past, as do many in our congregations), or labor in prayer for a lost world. We live as if grace has freed us from these Christian *duties*. Yet, in 2 Corinthians 8:9, Paul describes a very different grace: a grace that creates people who gladly become poor for the sake of others.

Still, we Western believers are tempted to think of the grace we have been given as a free pass into God's amusement park. We adopt an "eat, drink, and be merry because we are free in Christ" sort of ethos. In so doing we hijack the beauty and richness of God's grace and use it for self-centered living. In the movie *Hello Dolly*, Dolly Levi quotes her dead husband, Ephraim, as saying: "Money, pardon the expression, is like manure. It is not worth a thing unless it is spread around, encouraging young things to grow."[10] Although grace is nothing like manure, there is much wisdom in Ephraim's analogy. Some things are not to be hoarded. Grace loses its essence when it is stockpiled or selfishly spent. People who use grace to feel good about themselves and their selfish decisions will have an odor, but it won't be the fragrant aroma of Christ. They may pepper their speech with the word, but if they hoard that grace for themselves, it will become worthless. As we give away the grace we are given, encouraging young things to grow, the fragrance of Christ will be life to us and to others. God's grace is always given as a gift to enrich us *so that* we in turn may give to others. Grace is never to be spent selfishly. Its very nature implies giving. Jesus left the wealth of heaven to take on our poverty so that we might become rich. In his poverty he trusted his Father to take care of him. As believers we have the riches of Christ. As his grace works in us, it produces the same effect in us that we see in him. We spend his grace on others and trust our Father to take care of us, just as he cared for his Son.

Still, there are times when we don't believe that God will care for us in ministry and we hesitate to give ourselves for the benefit of others. This is usually the result of someone betraying our trust or wounding us. Nearly everyone in ministry has been hurt this way. When we respond with self protection, we fearfully hang onto God's grace for ourselves. We want his grace to free us from fear and guilt and duty, but we don't want that grace to create a servant's heart in us that compels us to pick up our crosses and give our lives for his kingdom. We are afraid that when God's grace looks like a cross in our lives, the cost will be too high.

On a dark night in Gethsemane, Jesus wrestled with the cost of salvation, yet he did not shrink back from God's plan when Judas arrived to betray him (Luke 22:47–48). Jesus knew what the day of crucifixion would bring, but he did not hesitate or waver. He trusted his Father. It is pitiful how scared we are of what God will ask of us. We are afraid it will be more than we can do, more than we can bear, more than we want to give. Before you know it, we are holding ourselves at a slight distance from him just in case we need to make a quick getaway. We say that we love his grace, but deep inside we believe the lie that captivated Eve. We ask ourselves, "Is God really trustworthy? Is he withholding some good thing from me? Do I need to step in and care for myself?"

When people use us, when circumstances are hard, when our marriages falter, when we are lonely, when ministry is not meeting our expectations, we are tempted to stop trusting in God's goodness and love. Our God is a loving Father, yet when life becomes difficult, we are tempted to believe that he is hardhearted, lacking any real sympathy for us. We know what obedience cost Jesus, and we worry because we forget who asks these things of us. God has shown us his love, mercy, kindness, and faithfulness. He has made us his children, sacrificing his own dear Son for our sake. Why do we fear him and worry that he will not take care of us if we respond to his grace and give ourselves away?

Giving up our rights and freely forgiving those who wound us can be hard to do. Yet ministry is full of moments that require just this. One young woman whose husband was fresh out of seminary and a new assistant in a large church shared her difficulties with me. The church staff was cliquish and she never felt welcomed into the group. There were many instances when she was wounded by their thoughtless words and behavior to her. She felt that God had given her the impossible task of forgiving, loving, and serving this group. She had already begun to harden her heart toward them when we met. In light of what she perceived as their low opinion, she just couldn't humble herself anymore by telling them they had offended her. The cost of taking the low place of humility before this cliquish group—who should have known better and welcomed the newcomer—was just too much for her. Even while she resented them, she found herself constantly worried about their opinions of her.

Fear of what God will ask of us has a powerful effect on us as we are in ministry. Fear creates worry. Perhaps we doubt that God will take care of us and those we love; or perhaps we are afraid that his expectations will be unreasonable and our lives will become drudgery. When our trust in him falters, we begin to take care of ourselves. We rebel by believing wrong things about God and turning away from him. In our rebellion, we question what God is doing and decide that we know better how he should run our part of his universe. But taking over God's role creates a constant undercurrent of worry in us. Our pride believes we can do a better job than he is doing, but our common sense realizes that our resources, powers of persuasion, gifting, and ability to control people and circumstances will only get us so far. Worry is the natural consequence. Sometimes it seems to spring up in every corner of our lives.

Perhaps you have never thought of yourself as judging God or thinking that you were smarter than he is. Foundational sins like wanting to be God are often invisible to us. When I first took the Sonship course[11] in 1991, one of the assignments was to ask several people this question: "If there was one thing about me that you could change, what would it be?" I decided to ask the question to our three children (then eight, ten, and twelve). I felt that their answers to Mom would be safe. Boy, was I surprised! Each of them in their own way told me that I was very controlling. I—their sweet, loving, always-thinking-of-their-good, sacrificial mother— was controlling? My bent to control circumstances, opinions, friends and, in their experience, almost every aspect of their lives, revealed the prominence of worry in my life. I thought my control was keeping the children safe and guaranteeing their future paths, but what it actually revealed was my unwillingness to trust God's love and care for them.

Mothers think we know what is best for our children. Christian mothers are certain we know what is best for our children. Christian mothers in ministry have elevated our certainty to divine revelation. We *know* what is best for our children. We are all tempted to grade God's performance when it comes to the things that are dearest to us, like our children. My tendency to maintain a high degree of control over our home life was the result of worry—which was based on the low grade I had given God for his care of us. I had judged him according to my expectations and been disappointed. Worry and the behaviors that result from it are indicators that we no longer trust God's goodness, willingness, and ability to care for us well.

> Therefore I tell you, do not be anxious about your life, what you will eat or what you will drink, nor about your body, what you will put on. Is not life more than food, and the body more than clothing? Look at the birds of the air: they neither sow nor reap nor gather into barns, and yet your heavenly Father feeds them. Are you not of more value than they? And which of you by being anxious can add a single hour to his span of life? And why are you anxious about clothing? Consider the lilies of the field, how they grow: they neither toil nor spin, yet I tell you, even Solomon in all his glory was not arrayed like one of these. But if God so clothes the grass of the field, which today is alive and tomorrow is thrown into the oven, will he not much more clothe you, O you of little faith? Therefore do not be anxious, saying, "What shall we eat?" or "What shall we drink?" or "What shall we wear?" For the Gentiles seek after all these things, and your heavenly Father knows that you need them all. But seek first the kingdom of God and his righteousness, and all these things will be added to you. Therefore do not be anxious about tomorrow, for tomorrow will be anxious for itself. Sufficient for the day is its own trouble. (Matthew 6:25–34)

As we read through this familiar passage on worry, it is easy to get distracted by the particulars (choices of clothes and food), which may lead us away from the passage's intent rather than toward it. How many of us have been taught that simplifying our weekly menus and cleaning out our overstuffed closets is the secret to a worry-free week—or encouraged that as we rid ourselves of stuff, we also rid ourselves of worry?

When we think of Jesus's teaching on worry through the narrow grid of simple choices, we can miss the heart of the passage. We can wind up creating new laws that will alleviate our worries: the laws of simple living. Perhaps we might create a new magazine entitled, *Jesus Keeps It Simple*. There would be a section of simple fashion choices that endure for decades, decorating with the simplicity of nature (consider those lilies), and ten meals to last a lifetime. And although Jesus says that worry will not add a moment to our lives, many have become convinced that the absence of worry will. We have been told that our choices give us the power to live a longer life, as if God were not in charge of our days. Wouldn't it be wonderful (we think) if the remedy for worry were as easy as cleaning out our closets, throwing away our cookbooks, and committing ourselves to a healthy regime!

Reading Jesus's words about worry brings another passage to mind: "For the LORD sees not as a man sees: man looks on the outward appearance, but the LORD looks on the heart" (1 Samuel 16:7b). Jesus is not critiquing our overflowing closets or the foods we choose to eat in Matthew 6. Nor does he say that we can add a moment to our lives. He is talking about the condition of our hearts. He wants us to examine where we place our trust, where our confidence lies, where we find fulfillment in this life. The things that cause us to worry are indicators of misplaced trust, but simplifying those indicators will not change what we are trusting.

Jesus assures us that he has everything covered, even the basics. We can trust him to take care of us in every way so that we don't get bogged down in daily worries, but spend our energy as a part of something bigger. He is working in this world to gather his people. He wants our attention to lie there rather than worrying about how we will meet our needs each day or pursuing pleasures as if they will fulfill us. We are not to fill our lives with things that will distract and derail us from his calling. His kingdom is our focus, belonging to him is our assurance of success, and he will take care of the rest.

The text ends by saying that our Father knows our needs, the implication being that he will provide for us. Just to make sure we do not make this passage the law of simplistic living, Jesus ends by telling us that each day has its own trouble. Following Christ often puts us in the middle of troubles we could have otherwise avoided. Many of us have been helped by simplifying life in this complicated world but we cannot always avoid trouble by making good choices. We face trouble by trusting God to take care of us. The focus of the passage is plain: Whom do we trust?

We are complicated beings. We were created with many facets and no two of us are the same. God created us for meaningful work and self-expression. Even in the garden, Adam was given the enviable assignment of choosing a name for every animal. He must have had found satisfaction in creating a name that fit each creature. Although sin has interrupted and twisted our experience of this, it is still the way God has made us. He wants us to express our uniqueness through our work.

Creating comes naturally to me. Although I don't have a garden of animals to name, I am constantly changing the things in my life. I rearrange furniture, change paint colors, and dream up new things to cook. I have a dear friend, however, who is very different from me. I'm sure my constant fiddling is a mystery to her. Her gifts are more administrative and organizational. Yet, when she volunteers to host a dinner, she feels an internal pressure to create a completely new menu for it. Our gourmet culture presses in on her. She often apologizes for what she feels is her creative deficit. But when she forgets the value of the gifts God has given her, her joy in serving is diminished by the pressure she feels to be someone she is not.

I, on the other hand, hate to be tied to the same menu. It feels impossible to stay on script. It's the way God has made me. But when I am around others who take a simpler approach, I feel guilty for the excess I bring to everything I do. God's creativity shines through our differences, which should be a source of joy for us. Yet often our differences lead us to worry as we compare ourselves with others and fear that we have somehow disappointed God or those around us.

We find so many things to worry about. We worry about failing; we worry about money; we worry about relationships; we worry about what we forgot; and we worry about what we will have for dinner. Ministry enlarges our circle of worries. We worry about our church plants and our ministry teams. We worry about support raising and church budgets. We worry about the people with whom God has filled our lives. We worry about almost everything! Yet trying not to worry, rehearsing facts to interrupt worry, and arranging and manipulating life to prevent worry are all ineffective ways to stem the tide.

Worry is a powerful force. The fall of man (Genesis 3) has hardwired us for it. Worry is a result of turning away from God to other sources for life and help. This turning away from God is what sets us up for worry, not our difficulties or our circumstances. Our culture has not helped us with this. We have been taught that material possessions and healthy living are our best weapons for a worry-free life. The sheer volume of information reinforcing this idea wears us down, and most would agree that a healthy bank account and a healthy body *do* decrease our everyday worries. But this is the world's way of dealing with worry—work as hard as you can to cover all contingencies and hope for the best. In contrast, Christ reveals a very different way to deal with our worries.

Jesus's answer is to remind us of our value to God, our heavenly Father. Because we are God's children, he will take care of us. He reminds us that worry is a waste of time, powerless to add one moment to our lives. Although Jesus points out the foolishness of our worries since we have God as our Father, there is nothing in the passage to indicate that he thinks we can reason our way out of worry. Instead, Jesus offers a way out that at first appears to be no answer at all. Jesus encourages us to seek God's kingdom and righteousness. How can this address our worry problems?

First, let's think about what happens as we seek his kingdom. When we involve ourselves in kingdom work, we see God working. We experience firsthand his promise to *add* to our lives the things we need. We find him faithful. We are privy to the answered prayers of others. Our trust in him changes from something theoretical to something more concrete. We learn to trust him better as we experience how trustworthy he is.

Seeking his righteousness has a similar effect. Our relationship with him rests on the solid ground of his work for us, not our work for him. We are confident of our perfection (Hebrews 10:14) as we stand before our Father because that perfection belongs to another—to Christ. If we daily seek to earn God's favor through a righteousness we produce, we can never be certain we have hit the mark and thus will have no confidence that he will keep his promises to us. We will worry. But when the righteousness we rely on is his and not ours, we find ourselves standing on solid ground. As we wear Christ's robe of righteousness, our capacity to believe he will keep his promises grows. His righteousness gives us a righteous viewpoint that we do not have otherwise from which we can believe and trust completely in the goodness of our Father. Out of the righteousness he provides for us, our trust in him will grow stronger and more certain.

A number of years after she and her husband moved to another church, I ran into the young pastor's wife who had struggled so much with the cliquish church staff. She confessed to me that she had never been honest with those who had hurt her. She had left feeling a deep sense of failure. But in the intervening years God had begun to work more confidence in her about her righteous standing before God because of her union with Christ. She had come to realize that her greatest failure had been her failure to love those who had hurt her. The constant worry about what they thought of her had prevented her from finding ways to enter their lives with love. Her way of coping with their lack of interest in her was to feign disinterest in them. She explained to me how her worries about her reputation as a spiritual person had distanced her from Christ and those around her. She was now more honest about herself and had begun to risk her reputation of spirituality. I saw a fresh willingness to put aside her needs to serve the needs of others regardless of their good opinion of her. This kingdom focus had come about because she was more certain of her value to God as a righteous daughter. Worry over her reputation had diminished considerably. She was learning to believe that she could trust God to care for her even in the difficulties of church ministry.

Being involved in kingdom work gives us greater access to the amazing things God does each day. The Spirit uses our experiences to recalibrate our thinking. The bigness of our God—his plan of redemption, his love for the world, his work to gather his people, his weaving of history and lives to accomplish his ends, and his power to do all his will has a life-changing effect on us. Knowing that we are the righteous children of a righteous God has a life-changing effect on us as well. Each moment we stand in Christ's righteousness is a moment free of worry. Being in God's presence, perfectly accepted by him, turns our attention to him. When we see

God through the gift of his Son, there is no need for us to worry. What wouldn't our Father do to take care of us? Look at what he has already done to demonstrate his love. These are the answers Jesus gives for our worries, but such big ideas and answers are hard to take in. One minute we have them in mind and the next minute they are gone. Paul describes us as "jars of clay" (2 Corinthians 4:7) and so we are.

Recently I had a weeklong worry marathon. Josiah and I were leaving for a six-week trip visiting multiple countries and staying in a multitude of places. I woke several nights worrying about what to pack, fretting about our need for an extra carry-on (because luggage is often lost on these trips) and the need then to drag two suitcases and a computer bag everywhere. I wasn't sure where or when I would be able to wash our clothes. When you are staying only one or two nights in each place, the no-clothes-dryer lifestyle of most of the world has an impact. Do I pack extra clothing? That seemed like a bad idea and took me back to the problem of too much stuff. We also had computers, power strips, and on and on. That does not even address all that had to be organized on the home front for our six-week absence.

Fortunately, two things happened to interrupt the worry stirring around in this jar of clay. One was a logistical chart I prepared for all the places and people we would visit. My thoughts were diverted from packing woes to God's work in the world and the dear people he is using to do it. I got excited about being with them and began to pray for my time in each place. Our many destinations were no longer problems to navigate but people to enjoy and serve. At the end of my week of worry, as I lay awake wondering where I would wash our clothes, I had to laugh at myself. We always find a place to wash our clothes! What a silly thing to worry about. The logistics of the trip overwhelmed me and I responded with worry. It was a relief to repent of each worry the Spirit brought to mind. I prayed, "Jesus, please forgive me for not believing that you would provide clean clothes when we need them. Please forgive me for not believing that you would give me the wisdom I need when it's time to pack. Father, please forgive me for doubting that you would provide grace for all of the travel, layovers, plane rides, waiting, early departures, late arrivals, bad-bed-backaches, and most of all, stamina for all of the relationships and conversations that will take place."

As an introvert and a detail person, it's easy for me to be overwhelmed by all of the elements involved in our travels. Saying no to my worries and trusting Christ to take care of everything do not come automatically to me, but when he interrupted my worries with thoughts of the work he is doing and then unfolded the particulars of my sinful response to him, he gave me a way out of worry. He supplied details on what to repent of and what to believe.

We can barely fathom what a worry-free day would be like. What would we do with all the extra mental space and emotional energy? So much of life is about managing worry, from the small moments of forgetting your password, to the bigger moments of wondering how you will pay a bill, lead a Bible study, love someone, or survive an illness. Jesus told us that every day has its own trouble. It is a part of life. The goal for a believer is not the trouble-free life that the unbeliever pursues, but a life that turns to Christ when trouble comes. As we trust him, he will comfort us and help us through our worries.

What Are Your Thoughts?

1. List your top five worries. What would have to happen to remove each worry from your list?

2. How have you organized your life to protect yourself from stress? How does that affect your ability to hear the Spirit?

3. In what ways do you use God's grace for selfish purposes?

4. As you think about your worries, what are you believing or not believing that gives each one power? Taking time to think through your answers may show you new ways to repent as you bring your worries to Christ.

Pause and Reset
Peace

And the effect of righteousness will be peace, and the result of righteousness, quietness and trust forever. (Isaiah 32:17)

I don't worry about speed traps if I'm not speeding. That brings with it a measure of driving peace. But obeying the speed limit doesn't help me when two semis box me in on the interstate or I have a flat tire or I see signs for roadwork ahead. Since we live in a fallen world, even perfect behavior is not enough to ensure peace. Something or someone is always intruding. Jesus, the only perfect man, was surrounded by turmoil much of the time.

As Christians we frequently confuse the promise of inward peace with the experience of outward peace. When Scripture talks about peace, our thoughts turn to a babbling brook running through shaded woodlands or a chair on the beach. We work hard to create places in our lives where we feel at peace. We unwind with a book or go for a run. We go to a movie or take a walk in the woods. We avoid people who are contentious and complaining. We use our resources to isolate ourselves from the fray and buy ourselves some peaceful moments. Although we know well that peace is a fruit of the Spirit (Galatians 5:22), we pursue more tangible expressions of peace to give us the breathing room we need. We look to nature and God's generous physical blessings for the peace that only his Spirit supplies.

One of the titles that the Old Testament uses to describe the Messiah is Prince of Peace (Isaiah 9:6). In many ways this seems the opposite of the descriptions of Christ's life we read about in the Gospels. Our Prince of Peace did not live a life of outward peace, and he often disturbed the peace of others. He was surrounded by controversy and hounded by demanding crowds. His disciples were slow to grasp his teaching. The religious leaders of his day should have been his staunchest supporters, yet seemed determined to pick a fight with him wherever he went. He was despised and rejected, scorned and mocked. Jesus described himself as homeless with no place to lay his head (Matthew 8:20). He was ultimately tortured and killed. Jesus did not live a peaceful life, but his life purchased peace with God for us.

As Christians we have a righteousness we did not earn by our good works or good intentions. Jesus bought that righteousness for us at great cost. We receive his righteousness when we identify ourselves with his Son. What does that mean for us? Simply put, God no longer judges our thoughts, our attitudes, or our actions. He has judged Christ for them instead. We no longer live under God's judgment and wrath. Jesus was the recipient of that wrath. Even as his death wiped clean our slate of sinfulness, so his perfect life became ours as well. Before the Father we stand righteous in His Son. God is at peace with us because we are in Christ.

In Isaiah 32:17 we read that righteousness effects peace. When we rejoined Serge in January 2011, we lived out of suitcases for a time as we raised support. I have talked about the daily upheaval our homelessness involved. As an introvert I am always looking for some personal space, so this turmoil gave me a fresh perspective on how well I understood Christ's righteousness. When I am not at peace, what does that say about my experience of his righteousness? If I know I have the righteousness of Christ, why am I not at peace?

Try as I may, I can never *reason* myself out of turmoil and worry and into peace. Whether stateside or overseas, ministry exacerbates the worries of life. If I am not resting in Christ's righteousness, recounting God's blessings and faithfulness is not enough to quell my fears or ease my worry. The two go together. Selling our house, living on the road, and looking to others to provide our missionary support kicked my neediness into overdrive. Disappointing donor reports, pressing correspondence, finding each night's bed, making healthy choices from fast-food lunch options, finding mental space and quiet time to write this book, driving and driving on the interstate, paying bills out of a suitcase—these were the moments of my days without a home. I had numerous hiding places for my Tums because I never knew when I would need one. Although the details of daily life were challenging and afforded little outward peace, my circumstances did help to keep me dependent on Jesus for simple everyday things. And even though I needed the occasional Tums, God blessed me with surprising peace in our tumultuous circumstances.

If life is going well, we have a sense of well-being that we think of as peace. Life is good. Relationships are working. Our car starts in the morning. The computer boots up. We know where we are going to sleep tonight. Ah, peace! But when life takes a bad turn, our illusion of peace is shattered. Forgetting that we belong to Jesus comes naturally to us. We instinctively return to carrying the weight of our needs. The extra burdens of ministry add even more weight, which threatens to crush us without the presence of Christ. When we don't believe that Jesus will take care of us, the worries of ministry can easily overwhelm us. If we forget that Jesus is our peace, the struggles we face will eventually rob us of any peace we might have been able to create on our own. I have had many conversations with women in ministry who have just given up. They have nothing left to give. They can't take the pressure anymore. The weight of people's expectations, tight budgets, endless meetings, old computers, and simple exhaustion exact a price.

Our ministry choices often put us in a place of outward turmoil. Many women live in tough places that afford little outward peace.

The daily challenges of a hostile country or a blighted neighborhood affect us. Others of us live in more peaceful circumstances, but may struggle with the money problems that ministry often brings or find that people regularly nitpick and critique us. Ministry is rarely a peaceful lifestyle in which to work and raise a family. If we seek peace in things that create a peaceful atmosphere, ministry will regularly discourage us. The peace Christ offers us is not found in the physical world but in himself as he makes his home in us. "For he himself is our peace" (Ephesians 2:14a). I find it helpful to remember that Jesus, the Prince of Peace who brings peace to our hearts, lived a life filled with turmoil. As we follow him, he may lead us to people and places that don't bring outward peace to us either. We may not live in peaceful circumstances among peaceful people, but he promises to be our peace, which is far better.

God's righteousness brings peace to us and produces the fruit of peace in us. The Spirit continues to bring this intriguing verse to mind. Worry, distrust, and fretting are the opposite of peace. Isaiah 32:17 asks us to examine ourselves to see where our faith rests. Are we resting in God's righteousness? Are we worried or are we at peace? As we battle for faith on many fronts, our peace is always at risk.

In what ways do we lose our peace? If we judge our worth by what we produce we will feel compelled to justify ourselves even though we know what Christ has done for us. With our standards unmet, we have no peace. Many in ministry experience the "Egypt syndrome" (see Exodus 17:3): "Lord, did you lead us into the wilderness to die?" We wonder if God is paying attention to us at all. When we aren't trusting in him, we have no peace. And then there is a cynicism that comes as a natural consequence of being a part of the evangelical community these days. Do you have problems with a lot of what the church represents to our culture? I do. When we sit in judgment of others as if we have no sin, we have no peace. God continues to use the difficulties of ministry to remind me how much I love my comfort and what a proud, self-reliant person I am. When the outward turmoil of ministry invades our interior lives, our tentative grasp of Christ's gift of righteousness is revealed. Yet we must be clear on this point: Our relationship with Christ never rests on our work, even the quality of our faith, but on the finished work of Christ alone.

So, even while we find ourselves in turmoil, we may also find ourselves spontaneously singing hymns and waking in the middle of the night overwhelmed with thankfulness and joy. These treasured moments are one way God overcomes our worries and fears and fills us with the fruit of his peace. Our relationship with him is a spiritual one we cannot engineer. It is his gift to us. Many times these moments bring tears of joy and an overwhelming sense of being loved, convinced that not only did Jesus die for us, but he is in that moment interceding on our behalf (Hebrews 7:25). Christ's work for us is powerful enough to interrupt even chronic sins like anxiety and worry. When we bring our worries to him, his blood will wash us clean and the effect of his righteousness will be peace.

> What can wash away my sin?
> Nothing but the blood of Jesus.
> What can make me whole again?
> Nothing but the blood of Jesus.
> Oh, precious is the flow
> That makes me white as snow.
> No other fount I know,
> Nothing but the blood of Jesus.
> This is all my hope and peace.
> Nothing but the blood of Jesus.
> This is all my righteousness.
> Nothing but the blood of Jesus.
> (Robert Lowry, 1876)

Chapter 10

It's Bad You Know

Bad: not good; unfavorable, negative; evil; wicked.
(Wiktionary)

DURING OUR SECOND missionary term in Ireland, we spent considerable time with the Missionary Apprenticeship team. This large group of twenty- and thirty-somethings was comprised of American and Irish individuals who were adjusting to life in cross-cultural ministry. We adopted as our theme song R. L. Burnside's blues classic "It's Bad You Know."[12] Ministry is fraught with difficulty and often brings out the worst in us. At one time or another, everyone on the team had learned to sing the blues.

Our dear friend Stephen, who preceded us in Ireland, gave us this counsel when we arrived: "Going into missions is like pouring Miracle-Gro on your sins." This was certainly our experience! We had no idea how much sin could come out of us until we tried to do ministry in a place where we were no longer competent and connected. Having a theme song that pointed out the "badness" of our predicament (while being really good music) made team meetings more fun. Our team did a lot of laughing, but that didn't mean we weren't serious about our work. Everyone on the team had given up a lot to be there. But one amazing fruit of the gospel is that we stop acting as if ministry results are up to us. We are no longer center stage. We stop taking ourselves so seriously, as if everything depends on us. Our only hope is that Jesus will come and work through us. Burnside's song was our humorous way to remind each other of our predicament: sinners doing ministry? "It's Bad You Know"!

If the prospect of ministry as the fertilizer that encourages our sin to grow and flourish doesn't make us pause, we must also remember that not only are we sinners, but we are also religious sinners. For those who are following hard after God (like our friends, the Pharisees of Jesus's day), our dedication and good works may prevent us from seeing that we are truly sick with sin.

I have a dear friend who has a very effective way of talking about her continuing need for Jesus, as a believer. When she stands before a group, she writes adjectives on a whiteboard: worried, critical, envious, judgmental, covetous, lustful, angry, fearful, discouraged, joyless, impatient, lying, grumbling, unforgiving, self-indulgent, idolatrous, argumentative, hateful, gossiping, prideful, controlling, selfish, etc. As she writes, the room falls silent. Then, when she begins to speak in her honest and humble way, no one in the room feels justified in their obedience. At least one word on that whiteboard has pierced every conscience.

One woman who had been deeply affected by the gospel told me how she had decided to be honest about her sin with those who supported her ministry. She was determined to no longer pretend that she had few sins to confess. Unfortunately, the folks to whom she chose to confess her sin struggles did not value her honesty. They were disappointed in her and felt she was no longer worthy of the support she had been given. Those of us in ministry need the wisdom of Christ each day as we open our lives to others. I admired this woman's willingness to lose reputation and support in her honest efforts to confess her need for the cleansing blood of Christ, but openness about our daily need for Christ doesn't mean that everyone needs to know every detail of our sin. The Spirit will give us the wisdom we need here. Although our sin is "bad," God is the first one and often the only one who needs to hear us talk about it.

When the Holy Spirit speaks to us, he always tells us the truth. In his gentle but unrelenting way, he shows us why we need a Savior for that moment of our day. We always need Jesus and he is always near. We don't need to be saved every day, but we need to be reconnected by faith to what is already ours. We need to be reminded of the sin remaining in us and we need to be reminded of Jesus's promise to forgive, cleanse, change, and use us to move his kingdom forward. As we take our sin to Christ, we will grow in our freedom from sin. Ministry pressures us to have it all together and can obscure our sin. Our good works and good intentions may also blind us to our sin, but Christ has sent his Spirit to help us.

As the Spirit reveals the specifics of our sin to us each day, those around us will not know most of the sin we bring to Christ, but they will feel the effect of our time in his presence. When I met one particular young woman, she was full of her competence and abilities. She was never wrong and had an answer for everything. It was hard to be around her for an extended period of time because her "rightness" was exhausting. We lost contact for a number of years, but the next time I met her, she had softened considerably. When I heard a bit of her story, I could see how the hard times she had been through had had a good effect on her. Those around her no longer felt continually judged by her. She did not need to disclose the sin she had discovered in herself over the years. It was apparent that God had used the difficult circumstances that her "rightness" created in her life (as well as other things) to show her that she needed Jesus as much as the rest of us. The impact of the Spirit's work in her life was evident.

Those of us in ministry often find it difficult to see our sin. And when we live our lives as if little sin remains in us, those who follow us will see little sin and need in *their* lives. As others follow our lead, the room will fill with hypocrites and we will be chief among them. Knowing our daily need for the cleansing blood of Christ for our own sins is the only remedy for the hypocrite, even the religious hypocrite. So how do we see our sin?

God reveals our sin through our relationship with him and our relationships with others. (And isn't that Christ's summation of the law in Matthew 22:36ff?) Often we feel the effect our sin has on those around us by their reaction to us. At other times they may tell us outright what our problem is. God's normal way of speaking to us is with quiet promptings (like my discovery of envy) and through his Word. A portion of his Word that never fails to school us in our daily need for the cleansing blood of Christ is his teaching on prayer in Matthew 6. If we want to see our sin, this is a great place to start. Many areas of sin come to light in Matthew 6:5–15: our shallow worship, our insipid response to God's coming kingdom, our desire to be in control, and our unwillingness to trust in his care for us. These reveal our failure to keep the first part of the law: love God. When Christ teaches us to forgive those who have harmed us, he is referring to the second part of the law: love your neighbor. If we want to see tangible evidence of our sin, we can start with our failure to love our neighbor.

As I pray through Matthew 6 and ask God to forgive me as I forgive others, frequently someone comes to mind. There is probably no area in my life that more clearly reveals my sin sickness and need for a Savior than my struggles with forgiveness. When Jesus taught his disciples this prayer, he had us in mind as well. As we think about his words, it may seem harsh for Jesus to link our forgiveness from God with our forgiveness of others. It doesn't fit with our notion of free forgiveness at all. (Not only does this prayer reveal my need to forgive someone it often reveals my anger with God for asking me to.) How can the gift of forgiveness be free if it is contingent on our forgiveness of others? No wonder we never feel quite forgiven; we all have people we cannot forgive. Our struggles to forgive certain individuals make it hard for us to understand what Jesus is teaching in his prayer. When we look at our inability to forgive some offenses or we think about the difficulty involved in what we are asked to forgive, we may hear the words of Christ as unreasonable and unattainable. But when Jesus connected our forgiveness from God with our forgiving of others, he taught us about the effect that God's forgiveness has on us.

A steady stream of God's forgiveness flowing through my life each day will give me the forgiveness I need for others. The two are always connected—my experience of God's forgiveness and my forgiving others. I am not saying that forgiveness is a physical commodity we get and then share. Rather, the power to forgive comes from regularly standing in God's presence with my sin and receiving his gracious welcome and free forgiveness. This simple act changes my heart, and it is the tender heart God creates in us that can offer forgiveness to those who have offended us. Just as with many things in the spiritual world, we give little thought to the power of God's forgiveness to change us. But when his forgiveness is actively present in our lives, we will not be able to resist it. Bringing our sin to God daily will keep his forgiveness fresh in our experience. It is the way of his kingdom: we sin and God forgives us; we are sinned against and we forgive others. This is the redemptive effect of forgiveness. Even when those we forgive remain evil or keep doing hurtful things (although forgiveness does not mean that we remain in an abusive relationship), our forgiveness shines as a beacon of hope in a dark world. Our forgiveness keeps us from being like those who have harmed us.

The power to forgive comes to us as we receive God's forgiveness. For those of us who struggle to forgive, this is a great relief. God does not require us to manufacture forgiveness. When we come to him, he always gives us what he asks of us. As we regularly take our sin to the cross, God's forgiveness flows into our lives. It searches out our sin and thereby grows bigger and bigger in our experience. God's desire in showing us our sin is not to condemn us (Christ was condemned *for* us) but to free us from sin's power. Forgiveness is God's daily answer to every sin that comes to light. Our lives fill with his forgiveness. When we as believers refuse to forgive others who sin against us, it reflects our unwillingness to receive God's forgiveness. It is evidence of our refusal to allow the Spirit to convict us of *our* sin and need for a Savior. The answer to the condemnation we feel when we fail to forgive is not to try harder but to ask the Spirit to show us *our* need for forgiveness and to fill us with the forgiveness Christ purchased for us.

If that is what God intends, why does forgiveness often feel beyond our reach? We find some people impossible to forgive. We get caught in a cycle of blame and guilt because their offenses against us often involve betrayal. Sometimes the wound is so great that we can't bring ourselves to name the actual offense; just naming it seems to diminish us. Part of the evil that was perpetrated against us is the lingering sense that we deserved the harm that was done to us, that we are not worthy of the protection God gives to others. Some of us are unwilling to forgive—we may feel unable—and end up carrying the heavy weight of our unforgiving.

As we try to make sense of wrong ways we have been treated and the evil we have had to endure, we can't help but ask why God did not prevent it. We believe that he is all-powerful and that nothing escapes his notice. We are taught that he is good and that his love for us is so great that he sacrificed his beloved Son. Yet he did not step in and save us from harm. These facts don't fit together. God's behavior confuses us. We would never stand by and allow our children to suffer this way! Where was God when we needed him?

It might seem like a harsh remedy to those who have suffered evil, but freedom from its hold over us comes when we admit that we too are evil and in need of a Savior. We who have much to forgive need to know how much *we* have been forgiven, so that our lives will be full of God's forgiveness. Then we will be able to for-give those who have committed evil against us. We will only have the courage to look at the dark places in our hearts when we are sure that, no matter what is revealed about us, every sin has been forgiven and we have been made "perfect forever" (Hebrews 10:14 NIV), by the blood of Christ. When we are willing to agree with the Spirit as he exposes the evil remaining in us, God's forgiveness will flow through us to bring light and healing to the dark places in our hearts. His forgiveness breaks the power that evil has over us.

I knew a woman who could not forgive her father. He had wounded her in many ways and, after she left home, she was con-vinced that the only way to be rid of him was for him to die. She prayed for this for several years. When God did not answer her prayers, she just avoided her dad and tried never to think of him. She got married, had children, and even became a pastor's wife. Because she believed she was nothing like her abusive father, she was very proud of the good person she had become. She could see little need in her life for forgiveness herself (although her theology of sin was excellent) but was an expert at pointing out the flaws of others.

When I met her, God had already worked deep change in her life. She was able to tell me her story because God had faithfully interrupted her perfect performance by bringing a series of cir-cumstances into her life that revealed that she was not a good per-son at all, but actually much more like her dad than she had been willing to admit. (She was controlling and used people to get what she wanted.) When God revealed the evil in her heart and her need for Jesus, she felt *her* need for forgiveness. After several years of a more realistic view of her sin and need of forgiveness, one morning she woke to realize that the process of forgiveness was finished. She had forgiven her father for the evil he had done. Although he died before she was able to tell him, she was released from the terrible burden that her failure to forgive had become in her life.

Forgiveness has a therapeutic impact on our lives. Its healing power will help us to function better and live happier lives. Yet there is a kind of forgiveness that is deeper and more powerful than our therapeutic efforts to forgive. This is the forgiveness that brought freedom to the woman whose father had deeply wounded her. When God is at work, the forgiveness he works in us forgives without regard for our benefit or how much those we forgive deserve it. The forgiveness he gives has a broader purpose. We forgive, not to free ourselves from those who have harmed us (although forgiveness has this effect), but to be a conduit of God's forgiveness in this world. We forgive to be like our Father who also forgives his enemies. Many times we resent the forgiveness God requires of us, as if forgiveness is our duty rather than a force for good. Forgiving is a way to resist Satan; it is our way to say no to what is evil and yes to what is good. Resisting Satan opens us to the presence and power of the Spirit at work in us and in the world. Forgiveness is one of many weapons we have been given to overcome evil.

When Jesus ascended into heaven, he left the disciples behind to accomplish his mission. Surely they wanted to go with him! Didn't they deserve to enter heaven with the triumphant, risen Christ? Christ loved his disciples yet, despite knowing all the ways they would suffer in spreading his good news, it was nevertheless always his intention to leave them behind. It is sometimes hard to get our heads around the fact that Jesus's plan for us is to live in a world that is evil (which is why we often spend so much of our resources creating heaven on earth). But leaving his children in an evil world is God's method of gathering his people. He leaves us behind because he loves the world (John 3:16) and is not willing that any should perish (2 Peter 3:9). Why do we think we can be involved in this rescue mission without being touched by the evil in this world? Just as God loved his Son yet sent him into an evil world knowing what he would suffer, so he loves us and sends us into that same world, knowing too what we will suffer.

The miracle of the resurrection is this: Though we live in an evil world, evil has no power over us. Although Satan is still "the prince of the power of the air" (Ephesians 2:2), he cannot destroy us. Jesus has entered Satan's (the strong man) house (this world) and bound him so that as we speak the truth of the gospel, many will be set free (Matthew 12:29). Jesus uses us to plunder Satan's house for those who have been taken captive. As we engage in this battle, many of us will be wounded, some of us mortally, but we are always safe in God's hands. When we realize that the power of the resurrection is at work in our lives (power for things like forgiveness), we are set free from the power evil has had over us. We are not crushed by evil, but see the evil that comes our way as an opportunity for the power of Christ to be displayed as his people are set free.

Forgiving the unforgivable and loving our enemies are the same weapons Jesus used to overcome evil. We, too, can overcome evil with good. Our encounters with evil enable us to enter the lives of those who have been crushed by it and bring them the hope and freedom we have found. Our words ring true because we are not speaking theoretically, but as ones who have experienced the power of Christ to forgive the evil in us as well his power to forgive the evil done to us.

Some of us pretend that we are the good guys who don't need the forgiveness of Christ each day. Or we stay in the dirt, angry and confused about what has been done to us. We have a choice in this evil world: Ignore the battle raging all around us or respond to the words of Christ to "Go . . . and make disciples" (Matthew 28:19), rescue the captives, and begin to push back the darkness.

Jesus laid down his life for his people. His disciples followed his lead. We are part of wave after wave of disciples laying down their lives for the next generation of believers. The mustard seed beginnings of Christ's kingdom have grown throughout the generations. As we take our place in this generation of disciples, we can trust that our encounters with evil will not separate us from our Father's protection and love or rob us of our faith. Just like the disciples before us, we will learn that Jesus's plans for us have purpose and meaning in this wave of gospel proclamation, regardless of what happens to us.

Do we think Jesus is sitting aloof in heaven when he sees our suffering? Jesus deeply feels our pain and the wounds we bear. He also experienced suffering at the hands of evil men. When evil intrudes into our lives, God has not abandoned us. This is where our sinful bent toward unbelief will rear its ugly head. With faith, we can believe what is true: God loves us. He is with us, working all things for our good and the good of his kingdom. Resisting the Evil One so that we might proclaim Christ is why God left us in this evil world. Forgiving those who do evil things to us is one of our most powerful weapons. As we forgive, we relinquish our right to retribution and revenge; we lay down our lives for another; we image Christ.

As Christ's messengers, we proclaim the gospel and present people with a choice. Will they trust the work of Christ for their forgiveness or will they refuse his gift and remain in their sin? We bind on earth what has already been bound in heaven (Matthew 16:19). "If you forgive the sins of any, they are forgiven; if you withhold forgiveness from any, it is withheld" (John 20:23). We don't have the power to forgive sins as Christ forgives, but we offer his forgiveness to a world that is under his judgment without it. As ambassadors of his gift of forgiveness, not only do we stand in his forgiveness for ourselves, we also offer his forgiveness in our dealings with others.

Understanding the power of forgiveness is essential to our comprehension of the gospel. A willful refusal to forgive pollutes our relationship with God; on the other hand owning our daily need for forgiveness and allowing it to permeate our lives changes us into those who are able to forgive. In this book we have looked at the sins of entitlement, envy, worry, resentment and our chronic unbelief as a few of the things for which we frequently need forgiveness. The power these sins have over us reveals much about our interior lives. Saying, "it's bad, you know" about our predicament is one thing—we can say it without owning it—but seeing that badness and its cost to God and those around us is quite another. When we get a real glimpse of our sin, we *will* be undone. Because we hate the moment when we realize that we are the evil ones whose sins nailed Christ to the cross, we often refuse to look honestly at our sin. Instead, we become experts at minimizing or ignoring it. When we manage our sin rather than confessing it, we are neither listening to the Spirit nor trusting in the cleansing blood of Christ.

If we respond to the voice of Christ with guilt and shame or denial and self-justification, the focus remains on our sin or our denial—it never moves to the cleansing, restorative blood of Christ. Regular confession of sin gives us a foundation of faith to move beyond ourselves into the lives of others. We are not merely identifying ourselves as believers of the gospel but we are living each day believing that gospel for ourselves. Our testimony of faith rings true because it *is* true. When we connect to Christ's work for us as a necessary daily experience, we are no longer stuck in the loop of guilt and shame or the loop of ignorance and denial. We can look at areas of sin like our failure to forgive and not shrink back from what we see, knowing that Christ has provided for even our darkest sins.

Just as the bad news about our sin is really bad, so the good news about the cross's power to change us is really good. When we look honestly at sin and trust in Christ's provision for it, the result is a clean conscience. As we confess our sin, the Spirit assures us of the forgiveness and righteousness Christ brings. The conscience is wiped clean. The price for our sin has been paid and our guilt removed. This gives us an answer when the Evil One accuses us of hypocrisy and hopelessness in our repetitive sinning, or when he falsely consoles us by comparing us to others who are much "worse" than we are. If we resist the temptation to believe his lies, he will flee. When we believe the Devil's spin on reality, we stop short of confession, which is Satan's goal. Keeping us guilty or in a state of denial prevents us from going to Christ. When confession of sin is a normal part of our day, we are less likely to fall victim to Satan's schemes to keep us far from Christ. Regularly taking our sin to Christ keeps our conscience clean. This is crucial to ministry. Unbelief, pride, doubt, fear, self-promotion, self-loathing, discouragement, and self-justification are all fruits of a noisy, accusing conscience. That is a lot of junk for the Spirit to push through! Don't give up your right to a clean conscience. Jesus paid a high price for you to have it.

We all have much sin remaining in us. Yes, we are completely forgiven and have a relationship with God because of the righteousness of Christ, but his sanctifying work in us will continue until we die or Jesus returns (Philippians 1:6). Many of us have been Christians for a long time. As *old* Christians we are often tempted to "make peace" with our sin. After all, we are not what we used to be. We have made progress. We have read books on how to change, gone through counseling, attended conferences—what else can we do? It seems pointless to keep thinking about areas of sin where we never seem to change. Some sin patterns are just too deep. We may ignore them, rename them, or just make peace with them, but we have ceased to confess them. These are often areas in our lives where everyone around us has learned to tread lightly because we have closed off all conversation regarding their impact on us and on those around us. We refuse to let the Spirit speak to us regarding them.

When I first heard the bad news that I was a critical person, I had a hard time believing it. It took much sweet patience and some concrete examples from my husband and children to convince me otherwise. Because I had always thought of myself as a nice person and was highly critical of those who were critical (ironic, I know), it took the gentle, unrelenting work of the Holy Spirit to reveal the deep patterns of criticism that were my natural way to get through a day. Regardless of how long we have known the faithful love of Christ, there is still within us a resistance to his Spirit and a deep desire to make our own way. Older believers need the cleansing blood of Christ each day just as we always have.

Those newer to the faith are prone to certain kinds of sin blindness too. They are often naive about their tendency to sin. I remember times as a relatively new believer when I couldn't think of any sins to confess, or the things I confessed did not seem all that bad to me like forgetting to have a quiet time or driving over the speed limit. The complexities of our hearts and motives are something we discover over time. It's common for younger believers to be critical of older believers they think have sold out to materialism or other sins they find particularly offensive. It never occurs to them that they too are sell-outs. Immature Christians often have a better read of others' sins than they do of their own; their sin is more theoretical than actual. Regardless of how long we have followed Christ, we all need the cleansing blood of Christ each day.

Our sinful natures are tricky. One way they trick us is to persuade us that we must understand our struggles and sins before we can effectively deal with them. This is a particularly popular notion in our culture. We read books for understanding. We go to counseling and conferences for understanding. Many of us believe that these are the source of lasting change. We have an amazing capacity for analysis and knowledge, which is a beautiful way we image God. But often the deep roots of our fallen nature are displayed in our belief that understanding will give us power to change. If we just have all the pieces, we will have the power *within ourselves* to forgive, or love, or stop doing this or start doing that. We trust in the purity and exactness of our knowledge and if we do not change, we blame the sources of our understanding. We follow a different teacher, find a better counselor, attend a new conference, or read another book. Sin always has a better way—any way besides simply acknowledging its need for a Savior. Our deep pride hates to depend on the work of Christ; it fights to prove its own ability to bring about change. Our sinful natures push us to believe that if we know enough, if we are committed enough, if we are hooked into the right sources, we can change—no Savior necessary.

Yet in our saner moments, we know this is not true. Books offer knowledge and insight. The wisdom of a counselor can be a great source of comfort and help. God may use courses like *Sonship* to renew our dependence on the gospel. These are just a few of the resources God can use, but we must not be confused: the power for change comes by promise. "And I am sure of this, that he who began a good work in you will bring it to completion at the day of Jesus Christ" (Philippians 1:6). This promise was made to believers before there were self-help books, counselors, or Christian conferences. It is the promise of Christ to all believers: "You can trust me. Put all the weight of your hope on me. You can believe me. It is true. I will change you." Not all believers have the same capacity for understanding or the same resources or opportunities for help, but we all have the same promise from Christ. He will complete the work he began in us. Though sin has marred us, Christ promises that we will be holy in the end.

What Are Your Thoughts?

1. What does Christ say to you about the people you have not been able to forgive?

2. Imagine your life with a clean conscience. What habits, relationships, or events would change?

3. What would you like Jesus to change in you? What do you think those close to you would like to see changed in you?

4. In Philippians 4:8 Paul encourages us to change our thinking. Imagine yourself as loving, joyful, at peace, full of patience, taking

advantage of opportunities to be kind, full of goodness, known for your gentleness, and a woman who can control herself. How does honesty about our sin and our daily need for Jesus create a fertile environment for the fruit of the Spirit to flourish?

Pause and Reset
Hope

For what we proclaim is not ourselves, but Jesus Christ as Lord, with ourselves as your servants for Jesus's sake. For God, who said, "Let light shine out of darkness," has shone in our hearts to give the light of the knowledge of the glory of God in the face of Jesus Christ.

But we have this treasure in jars of clay, to show that the surpassing power belongs to God and not to us. We are afflicted in every way, but not crushed; perplexed, but not driven to despair; persecuted, but not forsaken; struck down, but not destroyed; always carrying in the body the death of Jesus, so that the life of Jesus may also be manifested in our bodies. For we who live are always being given over to death for Jesus's sake, so that the life of Jesus also may be manifested in our mortal flesh. So death is at work in us, but life in you. (2 Corinthians 4:5–12)

How can God use us to proclaim Christ—we who continue to question his love as we stand in the shadow of the cross? We who struggle to forgive others after all that God has forgiven us? We who still find ourselves doubting that he will take care of us? If we are sinners, and chronic sinners at that, what good are we, really? In 2 Corinthians 4, Paul gives a clear description of our proclamation of Christ. He says that God will make light to shine out of darkness. He created the world out of darkness and now he spreads his kingdom in the same manner. His glory shines into our darkness to enlighten us. When we admit that we are sinners, the glory of Christ crucified for sinners shines through us. Our message is not a message of good works and principles for living, but of Christ crucified for sinners. His glory shining through our flawed and fragile jars of clay testifies to the power of his forgiveness, his righteousness, and his love for us.

Years ago Josiah and I were visiting some missionaries who lived in a very hard place. As I spent time with the wife, I experienced a little of her difficulties. Her house was cold. The city was made of gray concrete. The weather was overcast and gloomy. Few of the food items she normally used in cooking were available. She was lonely. Life was depressing. Yet when I met the small group of believers who gathered in her home, I was amazed at the joy and laughter and fellowship they had. I know this woman suffered to live where she did. Each day was a struggle and she had regular bouts of depression. She had to fight each day to believe that God had not forgotten her. She was a jar of clay, but I was privileged to see the band of believers that had gathered around the glory of Christ that was shining through her life.

God knows we are weak vessels. He is keenly aware of the destructive power sin has over us. We have been redeemed from our desperate situations and are being renewed daily by the power of the Spirit, but we are still clay jars, easily chipped and cracked and broken. Yet it is in these humble, weak vessels that God has chosen for his glorious Son to dwell, so that when his glory shines through us, there will be no doubt that the power displayed is his. The glory that was revealed as Christ was crucified is revealed in us as we admit our sin and need for him. We rob Christ of his glory when we deny and minimize our sin, making the cross a small and inconsequential thing. We are humble vessels, but God has chosen to reveal his glorious Son through us. These are our ministry credentials: we have seen "the glory of God in the face of Jesus Christ."

When we are afflicted, perplexed, persecuted, and struck down, we are not crushed, driven to despair, forsaken, or destroyed. Far from being signs of God's judgment for our failures, these things are evidences of something much bigger. We are afflicted, perplexed, persecuted, and struck down so that the life of Christ can be revealed in us. To bring the gospel to a dying world, "we who live are always being given over to death for Jesus's sake, so that the life of Jesus also may be manifested in our mortal flesh. So death is at work in us, but life in you" (2 Corinthians 4:11–12).

God reveals the glory of his Son through us, yet how often do we question God and doubt his promises when we are afflicted, when we do not understand what he is doing, when circumstances push us to believe that he has forsaken us, when we feel that we cannot go on? When we hold onto our lives and refuse to lay them down for others, we experience the trials of gospel ministry as evidence of God's unfaithfulness. But when we lose our lives for the sake of others, we experience the trials of gospel ministry as an indication that God is working through us to move his kingdom forward. Even as we are afflicted, perplexed, persecuted, and struck down, the glory of Christ shines through us. We may struggle at times, but we know the joy of his presence and our faith grows stronger when we understand the purpose of our suffering.

We die to ourselves so that others may find life in Christ. Forgiving those who harm and offend us is just one of the ways that we die to our rights so that Christ will be revealed through us. Laying down our lives voluntarily so that others may know Christ does not come easy or naturally to us either. It is only as we are filled with the treasure of Christ that our jars are not ground into dust by the opposition we face. This is why our experience of Christ must be fresh daily. The resistance we encounter will be relentless, always seeking to crush us and steal our faith. Having the Spirit point out our sin is painful, disruptive, and upsetting, but it is the way he strengthens us to withstand affliction, the perplexing nature of ministry, persecution, and his call to lay down our lives for others. Christ's work of salvation will overcome even our toughest sins and strengthen us for even the toughest of adversities. Standing in his forgiveness and righteousness connects us to our powerful and glorious Savior.

Paul's poignant description of the hardships of ministry is sobering. Yet we know that he did not quit. There is comfort in Paul's words to the Corinthians. Even in his imprisonment, he was rejoicing in the treasure that he, as a weak and broken vessel, possessed. After all he had been through, he was not crushed, in despair, forsaken, or destroyed. He was, to the end, laying down his life so that others might find life in Christ.

The thankfulness that flows from a forgiven heart produces a sturdy faith. When the Evil One wheedles his way into our consciences, we have a sure and decisive answer: Jesus paid for our sin; we belong to him. It is not our sin that makes us weak, but our unwillingness to own it and take it to Christ. Yes, when we see the sin that remains in us we can have only one response—it is bad, but we take no pride in our willful determination to keep on sinning. As Christ makes his home in our hearts, our sin will increasingly cause us grief and sadness.

As an older believer, it doesn't usually surprise me when my sin is revealed, but I feel a weight of sadness and a longing for the day of freedom. We tire of our sin. We see how our sin hurts others. We see how our sin pollutes ministry and separates us from Christ. We have a fresh experience of the cost of our sin. Our sin gets old. We are ready to be rid of it, once and for all.

When we respond in faith to the Spirit's work of revealing sin, each visit to the cross reminds us of how much God loves us. Each visit evokes gratitude and praise for the Savior who gave himself for us. Each visit results in a joy that only comes from being received yet again by our Father. The Spirit is our old friend and comforter and when we respond to his conviction of sin with faith in Christ's work for us, he fills us with the fruit of righteousness (Philippians 1:11). As we are daily freed from the burden of our sin and filled with fresh hope of a future without sin, we will stop hesitating to take the place of a sinner as we do ministry. The fruit of Christ's righteousness will replace the righteous reputations we are so quick to build for ourselves. The gospel we speak will be full of hope that one day the part of us that keeps on sinning will be done away with. And the hope we cling to will become a reality—at last, we will be like Jesus. "Beloved, we are God's children now, and what we will be has not yet appeared; but we know that when he [Jesus] appears we shall be like him, because we shall see him as he is. And everyone who thus hopes in him purifies himself as he is pure" (1 John 3:2–3).

Chapter 11
Identity Theft

Identity theft: the deliberate assumption
of another person's identity. (Wiktionary)

HAVE YOU NOTICED how quickly we forget that we belong to God? After all our gospel conversations, we still forget who we are and why God has left us in this world. I've found that the grocery store is a great place to see how quickly I forget about God and how much I need him. Perhaps you have not considered the dangers we face as we wheel our carts. Some of us may feel sorry for ourselves because we can't afford to buy the food we would like to eat. Others of us get grumpy because we don't like grocery shopping. (The joke at our house is that I am a creative cook because I would rather create a meal from an empty cupboard than go to the store to fill it.) Maybe you envy those who don't have dietary restrictions that make your cooking more challenging. Or you resent having to do all of the planning, shopping, and cooking yourself. Yet I think the greatest danger is when we stand in the checkout line where the magazines are displayed.

Even though I know they are not going to tell me the truth, I still can't resist taking a look. Why do I feel good when I see photos of overweight movie stars in bikinis? Or have a secret satisfaction when someone wealthy has a tragedy? Even if I avoid the tabloids, the women's magazines assault me. Each magazine has a stunning woman on the cover to grab my attention. Then there are the articles listed on the cover to seduce me into purchasing the issue so that I can learn new ways to control my curly hair or finally lose that extra ten pounds I carry around. Even the cooking magazines employ false advertising. Have you ever bought a magazine that promised the world's best apple pie only to be disappointed? I have. Each magazine promises happiness in some form or other—the dangers of grocery shopping!

The image I see in the mirror is a bit different from the photos displayed in these magazines. I have rarely seen a model on a magazine cover in an outfit that I could successfully wear. I am not thin like these models and have rarely been disciplined enough to get myself there. I like the *idea* of being skinny, especially when I am shopping for clothes—not so much when I am planning a meal or ordering from a menu. Most of us cannot eat whatever we want and stay thin, particularly if we are over thirty-five or had a few babies. Our metabolisms (and baked goods) conspire against us. Because of our culture's standard of beauty, we will feel better about ourselves if we are thin. It isn't fair or right; it's just the way it is.

What is this power our culture has over us? Women who are educated, successful, attractive, and generally content crumble under our culture's demand for perfection. Our identity is constantly bullied by it and much of what we experience each day conspires to bring the message home. The perfect woman may occasionally walk through our lives, but our usual encounter with her is through media. It is easy to understand why we feel compelled to fulfill our culture's representation of perfection when we are constantly bombarded with her image.

Because the standard for women these days is so laughably impossible, let's think about just how ridiculous things have gotten for us. The ideal woman is youthful, with her perfect looks often airbrushed and artificial in some way. Yet, despite knowing this, her image still haunts us as we gaze into our mirrors. These ideas are reinforced by nonsensical sayings like, "Fifty is the new thirty" because women who are fifty are now expected to look thirty. Culture's ideal appears to be fulfilled by being a sexual object and we are lured into thinking it will do the same for us. (Those of us who lived through the women's liberation movement find this both fascinating and horrifying—women seem to be objectified now as much as ever.) Our perfect woman has great fashion sense, although we have found out the hard way that a beautiful woman looks good in anything (as opposed to our many clothes-buying debacles). Her silky hair is shiny, her straight teeth are white, her long legs are lean, and her smooth skin is soft and wrinkle-free. No wonder our identities falter! Few of us have the natural genetic tools for perfection. We'd like to blame our culture for our identity crisis, but we are willing participants. Culture wants us to be beautiful; men want us to be beautiful; we want us to be beautiful. Everyone is in agreement.

A successful romance novelist was asked why all her heroines were beautiful. Her reply was to the point: "Why would I want to write about ugly people?" And why would anyone want to read about them? Her great success indicates that she has read our culture perfectly.

As if a standard of physical perfection within reach of those who work hard is not daunting enough, we are also inundated with the abilities and accomplishments of our culture's model woman. She keeps herself fit and trim and looks great in spandex at any age. The food she cooks is noteworthy and every bite a culinary delight. She can host a dinner party with ease. She engages a plethora of gourmet cooks for training and inspiration, albeit on television. Her home is tastefully decorated, subtly displaying her skillful ability with color and a band saw. (The modern woman has her own set of power tools.) The media present strong, successful, career women who are also beautiful. Those girls take no prisoners in the business world in their four-inch heels.

Then there are the supermoms in minivans with lots of happy kids who are glad to be onboard. These women never lose their tempers, have a bad hair day, or wear PJs to take their children to school. The perfect woman even displays serious martial arts abilities and can kick some serious . . . well, you know, while displaying her tasteful tattoo. She has no safety fears because underneath her perfect exterior is a highly trained ninja master. Our perfect woman eats organic, goes to the gym, and drinks vitamin-rich products because health and strength are her high values. She is expected to look beautiful and feel great no matter what her age. She has even learned to conquer the death of skin cells. She recycles, composts, and monitors her carbon footprint. In short, the high standard for women in our culture is ludicrous! Still, as women, our deep desire to be loved opens a door of vulnerability that no amount of success can close. We are seduced by the notion that if we make ourselves into the perfect woman, our deepest needs for love will be met. Although we may not buy the magazines in the grocery store line, we "buy" the values they are promoting.

As we enter womanhood, we try to be perfect in every way. To fulfill our career dreams, we must be perfect students with perfect grades. Whether or not we are searching for a mate, all young women know that pretty girls get ahead and plain girls have to work twice as hard to prove themselves. Whether single or married, we are captivated by the idea that if we can just perfect ourselves, we will be loved. As we get older, having been knocked around by our failures in life, we resort to renegotiation. "I may not look good in a pencil skirt, but I can make a mean chocolate cake." As we age, we learn the subtle art of camouflage dressing to hide our flaws and chameleon living to hide our inadequacies. Our obsession to be the perfect woman continues.

Why spend so much time describing our culture's shallow view of women? Most women I have met in ministry do not seem preoccupied with the craziness out there. They are living quiet, successful lives. But whether we realize it or not, we *are* vulnerable to the subtle seductions of our culture. We *are* affected by the values and images portrayed in those magazines. We won't understand what is going on in and around us unless we are aware of the power this absurd standard has over us and has over the women in our lives. We are *not* immune.

Missionaries have different experiences with culture's idea of beauty. Women who serve in East Africa and are thin find that they are not seen as beautiful in the same way they are in Western culture. An African woman with some weight is considered wealthy, healthy, and beautiful. It's the Promised Land for those of us who struggle with our weight! Women who serve in Western European countries are often stereotyped as those "overweight Americans" if they are not slim and trim. Western Europe has a tough critique of overweight Americans, and our missionaries feel this disdain at times.

Regardless of the cultural standards we live under as women, most of us do not meet them. The majority of us have some flaws mixed with more attractive features. Perhaps our nose is too big but our eyes are lovely, or we may have beautiful hands but our ankles are thick. There is a big difference between beautiful and attractive-with-flaws. Our desire for perfection makes us susceptible to the marketer's claim that this or that product or procedure can overcome our flaws. These ideas are powerful because they contain some truth. I *do* look better with a stylish haircut, a well-cut pair of trousers, and carefully applied makeup. Our desire for the power and love that beauty brings seduces us. Perfect bodies, perfect faces, perfect hair, perfect cooks, perfect athletes, perfect decorators, perfect moms, perfect career women, perfect lovers, perfect friends, perfectly beautiful in all aspects of life: In our culture, beautiful women *are* powerful; beautiful women *are* loved.

The cultural tidal wave that threatens to drown us is, for women, enmeshed in our image of ourselves. Each morning we wake to the pressure of renewing what is continually corroding. There is devastating power in our images of perfection. We feel like cultural outsiders when we look in the mirror and see little resemblance to our society's images of beauty. These false images orphan us from our Father.

Those of us involved in campus ministry know how beauty affects who gets a date and who is left behind. The "spiritual" guys in the groups I was a part of usually dated the prettiest girls. What are young women to think when even the Christian guys judge us by our appearance? One acquaintance was a strong believer and lots of fun—everyone loved her—but she rarely had a date. She didn't physically measure up to the beauties that surrounded her. Almost every Friday night she went into a tailspin of depression. Most Christian guys I knew on campus had a superficial appreciation of beauty. I knew another girl whose looks were stunning, yet she rarely dated either. She was constantly fighting to be seen for the person she was inside and not for the beautiful exterior God had given her. She hated being treated as an object rather than a person with a brain and a heart.

I remember the first time I saw a beautiful, young Diana Krall perform on television. What was so amazing about watching her sing and play piano was the passion she put into her performance. She obviously loved jazz and put her whole self into each song. When she was interviewed afterwards, it was evident that she was unaware of her beauty as she talked with infectious excitement and joy about the jazz music she loved so much. Diana obviously thought of herself as a jazz musician first and foremost. She had found her identity in the jazz community. When our identity comes from our place in God's family, we can be confident in our gifts and calling in this world and be comfortable in our own skin.

All of us would benefit from understanding the pressures for perfection we are up against, but as women in ministry, we need to get this. When our identities are tied to the opinions of others, we communicate the gospel less effectively. Our talk of *good news* should be reflected in its impact on our identities. The women in our lives need for us to be the voice of truth and sanity here. If we understand the gospel, we no longer live our lives under the burden of standards that must be met. We now live in the grace of God's favor. Because of what Jesus did for us on the cross, we no longer devote ourselves to achieving and maintaining a standard of perfection (no matter what its source). Instead we devote ourselves to a person, Jesus. We are freed from every standard of perfection because we have *received* perfection as a gift. As women who are confident of God's love and his perfecting work in us, we reflect the true nature of redemption and attract others to this gospel of freedom.

In God's economy our diversity of language, backgrounds, looks, talents, and personalities is highly valued. God has made us unique and as we flourish under his approval, we become the women he made us to be. Everyone in the new heaven and the new earth will be perfectly themselves, like no other. What a contrast to our cultures—even church cultures—that want to make us all the same. Women we live and work with need to hear this gospel clearly. Women who belong to Jesus *are* perfect. "For by a single offering he has perfected for all time those who are being sanctified" (Hebrews 10:14).

I have a friend who has carved out a ministry niche for herself that is unique to her. Everyone is attracted to her vivacity and excitement about the work she is doing. She is a fun-funky dresser who is comfortable in her own skin. Although she is not a perfect representation of our culture's idea of beauty, she is one of the most attractive women I know. Her identity is safe in Christ and her life is filled with passion for living out of the gifts and calling he has given her. She is a great encouragement to women who cross her path.

Jesus knew we would face pressures to conform to the ideals of this world and he encouraged us to think this way: "Do not lay up for yourselves treasures on earth, where moth and rust destroy and where thieves break in and steal, but lay up for yourselves treasures in heaven, where neither moth nor rust destroys and where thieves do not break in and steal. For where your treasure is, there your heart will be also" (Matthew 6:19–21). We need to take seriously the peril of giving our image away to the pressures of culture. As the Spirit assures us of our Father's identity and thus our own, we will wake fewer mornings with the desire to remake ourselves into a reflection of our culture. As the precious treasure of our identity is safely stored in heaven, the corrosive power of culture will lose its ability to steal our identities and rob us of the joy of being the women God created us to be. As the perfect bride of Proverbs 31, we can laugh "at the time to come" (Proverbs 31:25). I doubt I will look forty when I'm sixty since I didn't look thirty when I was fifty, but I can be certain that I'll be more like Jesus than I am today.

What Are Your Thoughts?

1. Describe your idea of the perfect woman.

2. What are some of the standards for women you have noticed from our popular culture?

3. What are some of the standards for women you have noticed in your church culture?

4. List a few standards that you feel have particularly harmed you. What effects have they had on your life?

5. How can we "lay up" our identity in heaven for safekeeping?

Pause and Reset
No Longer Orphans

But now that faith has come, we are no longer under
a guardian, for in Christ Jesus you are all sons of God,
through faith. For as many of you as were baptized
into Christ have put on Christ. There is neither Jew nor
Greek, there is neither slave nor free, there is no male
and female, for you are all one in Christ Jesus. And if
you are Christ's, then you are Abraham's offspring, heirs
according to promise.

I mean that the heir, as long as he is a child, is
no different from a slave, though he is the owner of
everything, but he is under guardians and managers
until the date set by his father. In the same way we also,
when we were children, were enslaved to the elementary
principles of the world. But when the fullness of time
had come, God sent forth his Son, born of woman, born
under the law, to redeem those who were under the law,
so that we might receive adoption as sons. And because
you are sons, God has sent the Spirit of his Son into our
hearts, crying "Abba! Father!" So you are no longer a
slave, but a son, and if a son, then an heir through God.
(Galatians 3:25—4:7)

The law was given as the guardian of God's people until the
time was right for the Messiah to come. The law was a hedge of protection to keep his people from being absorbed into the surround-
ing cultures. This time is referred to as the childhood of God's
people, lasting until the date set by their Father when they would
become inheritors. Although God's people were heirs to the promise made to Abraham, they were no different from slaves under the
law's guardianship.

Paul includes us when he says that we too were children enslaved to the elementary principles of this world. He describes our slavery as the observance of "days and months and seasons and years" (Galatians 4:10). For the Jew, Paul is describing their slavery to the Jewish religious calendar, one of the guardians that set God's people apart from other cultures in the past. Yet Paul describes these principles as weak and worthless now that Christ has come (Galatians 4:9). Before the time of Christ, these laws and rituals were the framework of obedience for God's people, but now that Christ has offered the final sacrifice for sin, our reliance on them would be an affront to God. It would be taking something that reveals our *need* for salvation and making it our *way* of salvation. It is a way of saying that Christ's sacrifice was inadequate. The law was given to keep God's people safe until the coming of the Messiah, but once Jesus came, the guardianship of the law came to an end. We are no longer subject to it.

Rituals and laws are not evil in themselves. It is what we do with them that make them destructive. Something as simple and good as reading our Bibles can become a ritual-law that we trust to make us pleasing to God. Attending church can become a God-pleasing ritual-law; so can particular elements of our worship services. Although the guardianship of the law demanded the outward obedience of ritual, it was never able to create righteous hearts. "For God has done what the law, weakened by the flesh, could not do. By sending his own Son . . . in order that the righteous requirement of the law might be fulfilled in us" (Romans 8:3–4a).

To the experts of ritual-law in his day, Jesus said these words: "Woe to you, scribes and Pharisees, hypocrites! For you clean the outside of the cup and the plate, but inside they are full of greed and self-indulgence. You blind Pharisee! First clean the inside of the cup and the plate, that the outside also may be clean" (Matthew 23:25–26). Whether our laws are secular or religious, the results of our dependence on them are the same: the work of Christ for the forgiveness of sins is diminished and deemed inadequate. To enslave ourselves to acts of outward obedience, even as believers, is a fundamental rejection of God's remedy for sin.

In Galatians 3:25ff Paul introduces the passage with a foundational idea: "Now that faith has come" everything is changed. What are some of the changes? By faith the guardianship of the law has come to an end; by faith in Christ we are now *all* sons of God. Paul's use of the word "son" inclusively is not a cultural oversight. There are times when I insert "daughter" when a passage says "son" to personalize my reading, but in this instance we will miss the implications of the passage if we do so.

As we read through the passage, Paul makes it clear: now that faith has come, men are not preferred over women. In Paul's world the master was superior to his slave, religiously the Jew was preferred over the Greek, in society men ruled over women, but now that faith has come, in Christ we are all equal. God's view of us is not worldly; before him we all stand as equals. When Paul says that we are all "sons" of God through faith, we know because of the previous verses that women are not *ex*cluded by the word "son" but rather *in*cluded.

Paul is overturning the conventions of his day. He is saying radical things here. Jewish men in Paul's day prayed a blessing that included their thanks to God "who did not make me a gentile . . . who did not make me a boor [a slave] . . . who did not make me a woman."[13] Women as heirs were unthinkable: a woman before God equal to a man—unbelievable, a slave equal to his master—what an odd idea, a Greek equal to a Jew in regards to faith—what a sacrilege! Even after the coming of the Spirit, in the early days of the church the Jews had a difficult time believing that Greeks were their equals in faith. These were all revolutionary concepts for the audience Paul was addressing and they are still revolutionary in many cultures today. Our baptism into Christ is the great equalizer. Everything has changed now that faith has come.

For Paul's original audience, the concept of the son as inheritor was completely normal. All of the father's wealth and position was passed down to his son. We might critique his culture as unfair and shortsighted, but we will lose the import of the passage if we reinterpret it according to our cultural bias. If we insist on inserting "daughters" into the passage, we will exclude ourselves from the position of honor God gives us. Christ is the firstborn Son (Colossians 1:15) and as such inherits all of the wealth, honor, glory, and position of the Father. It is not unusual for Christ as the firstborn Son to inherit his Father's kingdom, but the mystery that was hidden through the ages until Christ's coming was that God would sacrifice his beloved, firstborn Son so that we might become his sons and heirs. As the Spirit opens our hearts to this unfathomable truth, we cannot help but respond with our *Abba, Father!* We are sons of God not by birth, but by adoption.

We were sons of Adam born in sin; we inherited our father Adam's sin nature. But when the time was right, God, the eternal, Holy Father, came through the orphanage and chose each of us particularly because he loved us. "I want her; here is the price for her adoption. I want him; here is the price for his adoption." He gathered us in his arms and carried us home. We are part of God's family because he chose us and paid the price for us to become his children, sacrificing his own Son to make us his children and heirs. We are, of course, daughters of the King, but in regard to our status as inheritors, we are all sons.

After all God has done for us, why do we so often find ourselves back in the orphanage, alone and discouraged, having our identities once again stolen from us? This happens to me frequently. One minute I am full of faith, and the next I am worried about what someone thinks of me or impatient with the driver in front of me who is slowing me down. We are usually faithful in the big moments of life, but the character that produces hope (Romans 5:4) is built in the small moments of the day as we confess our unbelief

("Lord, I just realized that I am worried about . . .") and rebellion ("Lord, I am driving as if I am the only important person here and everyone should get out of my way") and return to believing whose family we belong to. We return to our Father's house.

As we think about our identity in this world, it is naive to think that God's opinion of us as perfect will be the opinion of those around us. In this world we will continue to be judged by our looks and accomplishments. Those of us who fall short of our society's ideal of beauty and success will continue to be slighted and over-looked in many instances. Beauty and success *are* power in this world. We will always be its victims when we forget the words of Christ to us: "I have said these things to you, that in me you may have peace. In the world you will have tribulation. But take heart; I have overcome the world" (John 16:33). This world is not our home and we are not defined by its values, although we are bombarded and judged by them daily.

"But for me it is good to be near God; I have made the Lord GOD my refuge, that I may tell of all your works" (Psalm 73:28). I have found that it *is* good for me to be near God. The constant demands for perfection from culture and church, life and work, are only quieted when we are with him. In his presence our imaginary perfect woman loses her power and we begin to see ourselves as God sees us: heirs of his kingdom, honored daughters of the King.

God loves beauty. It is evident throughout his creation. As we accept Christ's gift of righteous perfection and take our place in his family, we will mirror the Beautiful One to whom we belong. We can rest easy that all of the King's daughters are true beauties.

Chapter 12

The Magnetic Effect of the Cross

Magnetic: having the properties of a magnet,
especially the ability to draw or pull; having
an extraordinary ability to attract. (Wiktionary)

THRIFT STORES AND antique malls have a magnetic attraction for me that I find hard to resist—and all too evident when it comes time for us to move. I can cram a lot of items with *possibilities* into a small amount of space, which means that movers always underestimate how big a truck they will need to move us. Each time we relocate, multiple trips to the thrift shop are required to donate items that were never transformed into something useful. Others get moved to our next destination in hopes that their untapped potential will justify their space in the moving van. To me, the stores where I find these things are full of possibilities; they draw me through their doors like a magnet.

What draws you in? Some of us find it hard to pass a garden center or a bookshop. My husband finds it hard to pass an Apple store without stopping in to view the latest products. These are human responses. We are drawn in because these places are filled with interest for us. They get our creative juices flowing.

If we want to know whether the gospel is real in our experience today, it's easy to measure our human response to it. When the gospel captures our attention, we think about it, we read about it, we talk about it, and we think about it some more. The gospel has a magnetic effect on us and draws us in. To those who have been changed by it, the gospel never gets old or loses its fascination.

Years ago I heard a missions speaker who was at the end of his life and ministry. He had been speaking in churches for many years but he still got excited when he talked about his need for a Savior. Even after years of faithful ministry, he knew he didn't deserve God's favor, but he was thankful that God saved him anyway. It was simple and real and you knew that the guy woke up every day believing it. He was glad he belonged to Jesus.

When our experience of the cross moves from the theological (head knowledge) to the actual (life experience), we don't mind saying that we are sinners or needy or broken. Of course we are. That is why Jesus had to die for us. But that is not where we live our lives. Even when I have to repent repeatedly throughout the day (some days are like that), repentance opens the door for Christ to come in. The focus of the Christian life is not our sin or our repentance; it is living our lives in the presence of God.

I hope that as you have read this book, you have been encouraged to believe that God will give you everything you need for ministry. Having a realistic view of ourselves as sinners who need a Savior each day will keep us relying on his Spirit and address our hypocrisy. Seeing the work he does in us to make us more like Jesus will strengthen our faith. Talking about our struggles honestly is not admitting defeat. Those of us in ministry are under terrific pressure to get things done and look good doing it. We have donors and church members looking over our shoulders continually. In many ways our livelihood is connected to our performance. It is naive to think otherwise. The temptation to lie or shade the truth about ourselves even a little bit never leaves us. Most of us succumb to this temptation at some point in our day or week.

Sometimes those of us in ministry slide into roles and personas as we talk about the gospel in an effort to please those around us or gain respect. But when we do this, we make it difficult for people to see the gospel at work in a real person they can connect with. I was recently at a conference and was struck by how unreal many of the speakers seemed. When they stood at the podium, their voices changed and their speech patterns got weird. I couldn't imagine those guys changing a light bulb or cleaning out the garage. At the close of this same conference, a young church planter's wife came by our Serge booth and broke down with tears as she talked about how hard her life was. I had the impression that she had come to the conference desperate to find help. None of the good words spoken at the conference addressed her need or reached her heart.

I can't pretend to know much of what this young woman was experiencing, but I do know that Christ was presented in such a way that she did not hear him speak to her. She needed to hear of God's forgiveness for her discouragement and unbelief, his willingness to meet her and answer her prayers, and find hope that he would use her in the work he was doing. But this is not the message she heard. How do I know this? The gospel has a magnetic effect on believers. When Jesus is the center, when his work of salvation is the focus, we are drawn to him. We cannot resist him. We hear his voice. He binds our wounds and dries our tears. He comforts us. He gives us courage to follow him and fills us with faith. When we cloud the message of the gospel with our godly personas (be they traditional or trendy), its magnetic effect is interrupted.

There was a pastor in our town in Louisiana who wore a suit and tie when he mowed his grass. There were many theories about why he did this, but the most popular was that the only clothes he owned were suits and ties. Louisiana is hot and humid and the grass grows really fast, so we all figured that he must have had a hefty dry cleaning bill as well. This pastor was actually a dear man who had a reputation for preaching the gospel but the community referred to him as "the preacher." His coat and tie had set him apart from the rest of the grass mowers.

Wouldn't it be great if those of us in ministry were able to blend in with the crowd and meet people where they live instead of becoming a strange subset of our culture? Just as my Irish friend could spot an American a block away, so most of us can pick the preacher out of a crowd. Why is that? Well, the reason might not be sinful, but sometimes it is. Most of us in ministry love recognition whether or not we are preachers. We may even use ministry as a way to build a reputation for ourselves. All of this pollutes the message of the gospel and separates us from the very people we are speaking to. It is just that simple.

As we read the Gospels, we never see Jesus acting falsely. He eats dinner with Pharisees and tax collectors alike. He doesn't slight women and even crosses the boundaries of propriety by speaking with a Samaritan woman (John 4:7) and allowing "a woman of the city, who was a sinner" (Luke 7:37) to wash his feet with her tears. Isaiah describes the Messiah very differently from the religious leaders of Jesus's day—and our day as well: "he had no form or majesty that we should look at him, and no beauty that we should desire him" (Isaiah 53:2b). Jesus was not a handsome trendsetter. As we follow his steps through the Gospels, we realize that Jesus did not cultivate relationships with the influential people of his day just because they were influential, although surely he could have made a great argument for doing so. Jesus did not avoid sinners; in fact, sinners were the folks he came to spend time with.

Ministry will take us to some strange places and introduce us to some unlikely people. As we follow Christ, we will find ourselves having conversations with those in society we may have otherwise ignored and in unexpected places not of our making (Josiah and I once had a luncheon Bible study in a corner office of the Rothschild Bank in Geneva with a pastor, a banker, and a billion dollar money trader). Many may not appreciate how we spend our time or why we have the friends we do. Taking the gospel to the nations will look different for each of us, but all of us should reflect Christ's humility and willingness to enter the lives of the lowest in society as well as speak the gospel with boldness to those who are wealthy and powerful.

Although the world is a broken place full of broken people, Jesus promises that he is making everything new. When we speak the gospel, we will not give a true account if we fail to communicate the hope of new life that it brings to us and to the world. That is why we are able to laugh and tell jokes, have cookouts and enjoy good music. Jesus is making everything new. The struggling church planter's wife needed to hear the whole gospel: forgiveness, righteousness, and new life in the Spirit. God works all of these in us. The gospel brings with it anticipation, not only of our freedom from the bondage of sin, but also our lives conformed to the image of Christ—the unpredictable Jesus we read about in the Bible.

The imprint of his image in us becomes more apparent as his Spirit works to transform us. When our love is genuine, our joy apparent, our peace steady, our patience visible, our kindness evident, our goodness forthright, our gentleness true, and our self-control visible to others, doors of ministry open as people see Jesus in us. Much of what is attractive about us to those who don't know Christ is the overflow that springs from this deep work of the gospel in us.

While the Spirit is working the fruits of righteousness through our lives, he is also equipping us for the good works God ordained for us to do (Ephesians 2:10). I used to feel condemned when I read that God had prepared good works for me to do, because I was convinced that I could never do them all. I did not understand that the gifts he equips us with to do those good works bring a lot of joy and satisfaction into our lives.

I have a gift of hospitality. Although I hate grocery shopping, I still love to plan and do the work that makes for a good party. During one large get-together, someone asked me why I had made so many desserts. I wasn't sure how to answer—I had had so much fun creating them that it never occurred to me that I could have made fewer. Hospitality is a gift and a tool I use for ministry. It creates a space for relationships to grow, resulting in gospel opportunities. The fact that it is a gift makes using it deeply satisfying, even when it's time to wash the dishes. All God's gifts are good and we find joy in using them. The combination of gifts he gives each of us makes us the unique individuals that we are.

Although some of us may be unsure of our gifts, God uses our willingness to interact with people (both inside and outside the church) and to try new things to reveal the gifts and abilities he has given us. We discover our gifts in the midst of relationships and activity, not in the quietness of self-examination. Trying new things may reveal gifts we did not know we had. Interacting with a variety of people may show us new ways to think about ourselves. We all struggle with the fear of appearing incompetent, but we will miss gifts that bring us joy and satisfaction if we give in to our fears. Feeling foolish at times is a normal part of life—it keeps us from taking ourselves too seriously! Discovering the gifts and abilities God has given to equip us for ministry is a lifelong adventure that will bring us joy and a deeper understanding of the creativeness of our Creator.

The power of the gospel is at work in us (Romans 1:16). As the gospel works its way through each area of our lives, our experience of Christ's love will deepen and we will be better equipped to handle the challenges that ministry brings. We all have days when we stomp around our kitchens in frustration. We all have days when we need to hide away and cry because we are overwhelmed and sad. We all have situations that cause us to raise our hands in surrender at the mess before us. We all know people we wish would disappear. Christ's love pushes us into a broken world, but that love also pushes its way into our hearts and makes its home in us. His love gives us hope for ourselves and for others. That hope is evidence that the gospel is at work.

As we grow in faith, believing that Christ is at work in the world, our eyes are opened to see it. Jesus will take us to people and places beyond our comfort zones so we can see what he is doing. Ministry is not just challenging, it is a door to blessing and adventure. We all have days when we dance for joy because someone who seemed beyond Christ's reach responds to him. We all have moments when we need to hide away and cry because we are overwhelmed with God's kindness and love. We all find ourselves in situations that cause us to raise our hands in praise when impossible prayers are answered. We all know people who are the dearest and most encouraging friends we could ever imagine. These are just some of the blessings of ministry. Although ministry puts us in harm's way, it also puts us in the path of great blessing as we experience Christ's powerful gospel at work in this world. Faith flourishes in a heart that is worked on by this powerful gospel. Thanksgiving and praise are quick to follow.

What Are Your Thoughts?

1. What about God is captivating your attention today?

2. In what ways would you like to see the gospel change you?

3. In what ways does Christ's love for you equip you for ministry?

4. What have you seen Christ do recently? How has it strengthened your faith?

5. Consider praying, "Jesus, open my eyes today to see what you are doing all around me."

Pause and Reset
Strength and Wisdom

Finally, be strong in the Lord and in the strength of his
might. Put on the whole armor of God, that you may be
able to stand against the schemes of the devil. For we do
not wrestle against flesh and blood, but against the rulers,
against the authorities, against the cosmic powers over
this present darkness, against the spiritual forces of evil in
the heavenly places. Therefore take up the whole armor
of God, that you may be able to withstand in the evil
day, and having done all, to stand firm. Stand therefore,
having fastened on the belt of truth, and having put on
the breastplate of righteousness, and, as shoes for your
feet, having put on the readiness given by the gospel of
peace. In all circumstances take up the shield of faith,
with which you can extinguish all the flaming darts of
the evil one; and take the helmet of salvation, and the
sword of the Spirit, which is the word of God, praying at
all times in the Spirit, with all prayer and supplication.
To that end keep alert with all perseverance, making
supplication for all the saints. (Ephesians 6:10–18)

We have looked at the gospel from various angles—through the
lens of a pastor's wife and a missionary, and from the perspective of
a campus worker and those who work for the church. We've looked
to the gospel for our new identity and the answer to the many sins
that remain in us. We've seen the magnetic effect it has in our lives
as it draws us into fellowship with the Father, Son, and Spirit. As
we end our gospel conversation, Paul gives us clear instructions on
how to remain faithful and not become a casualty of battle. This is
great advice for all believers but much-needed advice for those of
us in ministry. Many of us are tired and lonely, discouraged and

about to give up, but even those of us in ministry who are functioning well have to put on our gospel gear each day. No one is immune from the schemes of the Devil.

When I was a teenager in the late sixties and early seventies, there were several Christian movements afoot. One was the Jesus Movement, which focused on spiritual experiences. What validated a Christian's testimony was the flavor and intensity of these experiences. Denominations were viewed as divisive. The great thing about this movement was that it pushed people out of institutional expressions of faith into relational ones. The focus was on being a follower of Christ, one of Jesus's people. It was a fun time for a teenager to be a believer. We could rebel against the religion of our parents and feel righteous in our spirituality all at the same time! We also created some great music. It had been a long time since the music of the church leapt from popular culture. There were rifts in the church over music style and expressions of worship.

Sound familiar? Disagreements don't seem to change much from generation to generation. The schemes that the Devil uses today are just an update of the schemes he used in the past. Now as then, the temptation is to see ourselves as those on the spiritual "edge" and to judge those who are not with us. Those of us in ministry are often guilty of leading folks to the latest edge. There is always a new movement and a new edge to stand on.

The edge is where we concoct new laws of spirituality that we use to judge ourselves and others, and so fall victims to the Devil's schemes. There are many edges of spirituality these days: Are you grace-centered? Do you use our specialized Christian vocabulary? Are you worshiping with the majesty of a pipe organ to reflect God's glory, or is your music more in sync with the times? What Bible translation do you use? Do you exercise your free-in-Christ right to drink and smoke? Have you returned to true worship through liturgy? Do you sport an urban vibe? Are you committed to community? Do you dress in your best clothes for God, or come as you are on Sunday mornings? Do you express your beliefs with tattoos or bumper stickers? What is your missional philosophy in our new global community? It is crazy out there!

We are amazingly naive as we create our new laws of spirituality and succumb to the Devil's schemes. We look to the outward appearance of people and things—we always have. That's what sinners do. We have outward criteria by which we judge. But God is not like us. God looks at hearts. In stark contrast to our new "laws" of freedom and spirituality, Paul speaks simple truth to us. "Be strong and prepare for battle." He pulls back the curtain to say, "This is what you are up against. I want you to withstand evil and, when it is all over, I want you still standing." It's easy to critique the Christianity of others and think that our insights have more depth, truth, and in the current lingo, authenticity. It is easy to see the sins and mistakes of others and be blind to our own. Paul brings us back to the spiritual reality that Christians have always faced. We are in a battle and we had better put on our gear.

What would it look like to suit up for battle? In reading through Ephesians 6, we see that each element of the soldier's equipment points to the Spirit's testimony regarding the person and work of Christ. The Spirit will reveal Christ to us and, in Christ, we will find everything we need to fight the battle and be found standing at the end. We are back to the gospel. The finished work of Christ is our battle gear. We just need to put it on.

"And, as shoes for your feet, having put on the readiness given by the gospel of peace" (Ephesians 6:15). I have a weakness for shoes and must confess to having bought shoes for looks rather than comfort. But in the spiritual arena wrong footwear risks more than sore feet at the end of the day. If we are to stand against the schemes of the Devil, we need to put on our gospel-of-peace shoes that will keep us at the ready. The gospel brings the peace of forgiveness and a clean conscience, peace that today we have done enough, peace with God. Although we strive outwardly, inwardly we have peace, that solid-as-a-rock, unshakable peace that will come as we believe that the finished work of Christ is for us. When arrows start flying, that peace will keep us standing. When our peace depends on the opinions of others or outward circumstances, the enemy will take us by surprise and we will be the first to fall. The battle rarely begins in a recognizable form; more often than not, we are minding our own business one minute and asking ourselves how we got into this mess the next. We have to be ready before the moment comes, so that we are not its first casualties. The peace that comes from resting in the work of Christ readies us for the fight. Our gospel shoes give us a firm foundation for battle.

The belt of truth and the breastplate of righteousness are also aspects of the gospel. "Stand therefore, having fastened on the belt of truth, and having put on the breastplate of righteousness" (Ephesians 6:14). It is interesting to note that truth is not represented as a sword, knife, spear, or other sharp object. In other words, truth is not a weapon we use against others. Truth holds up *our* spiritual trousers!

Many of us are afraid of truth because we are not secure in Christ's work for us. As a result, we don't handle criticism well. But if the Spirit is active in our lives, he will be criticizing and comforting us day in and day out. That is his work: to show us our sin and to show us Christ's provision for it. A steady diet of truth will produce spiritual vitality in us. Knowing that our sin is covered by the blood of Christ will protect us from the Devil's accusations. What can he say that we haven't already heard? Our ability to hear truth is linked to our confidence that we stand in the righteousness of Christ. His righteousness secures us a permanent welcome into God's presence and a place in his family. As we believe the truth of the gospel and trust that Christ's righteousness counts for us, we will not succumb to the evil that threatens to overwhelm us. Although some may think that our openness about our sin makes us weak, honesty about our remaining sin keeps the cross fresh in our experience and makes us strong.

Faith is the shield we use in battle to protect ourselves from harm. "In all circumstances take up the shield of faith, with which you can extinguish all the flaming darts of the evil one" (Ephesians 6:16). What we choose to believe each day about Christ's work for us will determine how effective our shield will be at extinguishing the Devil's flaming accusations. If our faith is firmly grounded in Christ's work for us, the enemy's darts will be easily extinguished. What could the Devil say that is more difficult to hear than that our sins were the cause of Christ's suffering and death on the cross? As he points to our sin and failure, the news of our sin is not news to us. When we regularly go to the cross for forgiveness and cleansing, his taunts have no power over us. If even a little of our faith is in our good works or power to change, the Devil's arrows will wound and weaken us. Only our faith in Christ's work alone will be the strong shield that can protect us.

"And take the helmet of salvation" (Ephesians 6:17a). God has given us a helmet and it is a big one. Our helmet encompasses the whole plan of salvation. It includes the inception of God's plan of salvation in eternity past; the history of salvation that begins in Genesis and runs through Scripture; our own personal justification, sanctification, and glorification; and even the salvation of creation when Jesus returns. Paul uses all-encompassing language as he talks about salvation, the whole armor of God, and the evil that surrounds us. He paints the big picture for us. The evil we are up against is vast, but the salvation that protects us is even greater. Putting on the helmet of salvation identifies us as belonging to Christ and safe under his protection.

Lastly, we are given a weapon, "and the sword of the Spirit, which is the word of God, praying at all times in the Spirit, with all prayer and supplication" (v. 17). We are given the same sword the Spirit uses. Our weapon is Scripture. It is easy to see how the Bible has been wrongly used as a bludgeon rather than a sword. Quoting verses to win an argument for our own ends is self-serving and will keep us on the sidelines. So how are we to use our sword?

How did Christ? He knew the Scriptures and understood their meanings. He quoted the Scripture from a *biblical* viewpoint. He used Scripture to answer the Devil when he was tempted and to answer the religious leaders who opposed him. As we read through the Gospels, Acts, and the Epistles, we find that the writers quote the Old Testament throughout. We should not be afraid to quote Scripture to others, but knowing that God's Word is a powerful weapon should give us pause. If we quote Scripture to prove a point or manipulate someone's behavior, we are imitating the Devil, who quoted Scripture to tempt Christ. This is why Paul ends the sentence that began in verse 16 with a simple exhortation: Pray, "Pray at all times in the Spirit" (Ephesians 6:18). We have a powerful weapon in our hands. Appeal to God for help. We must not pick up our swords casually. We can do a lot of damage as we slice the air. Only when our feet are firmly planted in gospel humility and we have asked God for help should we pick up our swords for battle.

Are these ideas too big for the everyday? Is our armor only for special occasions? Paul's frequent use of the word "all" shows us that indeed our *gospel gear* is designed for everyday use: *all* circumstances (v. 16), *all* the flaming darts (v. 16), "praying at *all* times in the Spirit, with *all* prayer and supplication" (v. 18), keep alert with *all* perseverance (v. 18), praying for *all* the saints (v. 18). Living out this passage daily may feel daunting to most of us. There is a lot of equipment to put on as we dress for battle each day! How can we remember it all? What about all the praying that needs to be done? How can we possibly get around to it? The passage seems incongruous when seen through our everyday experience. Peace shoes for war? Ordinary people who stand against cosmic powers and spiritual forces of evil? It is no wonder that so many of us substitute a more manageable and realistic approach to ministry!

Cosmic forces are a lot to prepare for each morning, even after our first cup of coffee. Can we really become the soldiers Paul describes in Ephesians 6?

We may not look like much of a threat as we care for children, meet for coffee, and work at our computers but Ephesians 6 says that we are. Women can be mighty warriors on the spiritual battlefield. Whether we disciple women on a campus or oversee the women's ministries of a church; whether we are pastors' wives or missionaries; whether artists, teachers, doctors, or administrators, all women in ministry can be mighty warriors on the battlefield.

Ephesians 6 answers our deep longing to be part of something that will count for eternity. The gospel "is the power of God for salvation to everyone who believes" (Romans 1:16). Paul encourages us to believe this gospel for ourselves. He wants our thoughts and emotions to daily connect with the truth of Christ's work in us. Yet this is only our battle preparation. The battle itself is for those who do not yet know him. The particulars of the passage will be meaningful and helpful as the Spirit brings them to our minds (some of the "grace to help in time of need" for which we pray in Hebrews 4:16). By suiting ourselves in the gospel of Christ, we trust the Spirit to do his work. We expect that as we go into battle, he will be with us.

Paul mentions the Devil's schemes that threaten to discourage, overwhelm, and distract us. We need never fear them, but we need to be aware that Satan is constantly plotting against us. Church people (some Christians, some not) are often players in these schemes (some unwittingly, some not). Sometimes it feels like there is no end to the damage that some *church people* can do. The Devil is out to destroy the church and he often uses church people to disillusion us, distract us, and rob us of our faith. His plots to sideline us from the battle may include difficult circumstances, chronic health problems, loneliness, family troubles, our worldly desires, and even the good gifts and abilities God has given us, when we trust them for ministry. But Satan's schemes are only effective when we lose our connection with Christ's work of salvation. Our only hope of overcoming evil with good is to stand firmly in our gospel armor each day. As we focus on the gospel, we will be increasingly affected by the deep love behind it. We will believe it for ourselves and then be ready to face the Devil's schemes against us.

Lastly, we are to be vigilant and alert in our persevering prayers for all the saints "with all prayer and supplication. To that end keep alert with all perseverance, making supplication for all the saints" (Ephesians 6:18). God will hear our prayers and move his kingdom forward through them. It may appear shortsighted on his part to work this way, since we often resemble the disciples who fell asleep in the garden when Jesus asked them to stay awake and pray. Our inability to persevere in prayer shows a weakness of faith, but our prayers will get bolder, more frequent, and more outward-focused as the gospel does its work in us. Christ will change even this seemingly hopeless weakness common to so many of us. He will teach us to pray.

Christ provides everything we need to keep standing on the battlefield, and often his provisions for us include a friend. Most of us feel our need to have at least one other ministry woman in our lives. Few others will understand the difficulties and temptations we face. Identifying safe relationships and making time to cultivate them can be challenging. It is the one thing that continually gets bumped from our to-do list. We know that there is potential for all sorts of messiness if we confide in women who might later gossip about us. This fear often derails our search for a faithful friend. Asking God to provide a small group of women we can trust should be at the top of our prayer lists. These needs are not selfish, but a reflection of the spiritual danger we face when we keep ourselves isolated and alone. We all need to hear Jesus's voice through the encouragement of other sisters in ministry.

Jesus calls women to put on our battle gear and step onto the field. It is time to stop worrying about our lives and our readiness for battle. Christ is always with us. There will never be a day when we won't be humbled by our failure to do the simple things Jesus asks of us or a day we won't need his cleansing blood. But the more we return to the cross, the more powerful its draw will be on us. Repentance ushers us into God's presence where we find relief from trouble and joy in hardship.

The cross is where we hear Christ's assurance that his work of salvation for us is finished. Those who do not see their need for a Savior think of our preoccupation with the cross as weak and weird, but to those of us who see our need of a Savior, the cross is everything. It is God's most powerful communication of love to us. "For God so loved the world, that he gave his only Son, that whoever believes in him should not perish but have eternal life. For God did not send his Son into the world to condemn the world, but in order that the world might be saved through him" (John 3:16–17). The power of God's love and Christ's work of redemption will change us deeply as we believe they are for us. As he convinces us of these truths for ourselves, the Spirit will give us courage to fight for the faith of others. Through us God will love the world, and through us he will save the world by the work of his Son.

Perhaps these ideas don't feel like enough of an answer to the hardships of ministry. For many years I looked for a Christian manual that would tell me what to do in every situation. I wanted a book that gave me the how-to of ministry life. But eventually I learned through experience that there is no case law big enough to cover our response to all of the people and situations we encounter. We can encourage one another with the wisdom we have gleaned over the years, but nothing will replace the work of the Holy Spirit to change hearts, minds, attitudes, and circumstances and to open new doors of ministry for us.

Living our lives transparently so that others can see the gospel at work in us is humbling. Some will use our openness against us.

Our willingness to die to our reputations will make us vulnerable and keep us praying. The hardships of ministry can be a great gift to us if our solution is to run to Jesus. Our spiritual lives will be rich if this is our habit of life.

When Jesus chooses us for ministry, he effectively takes everything from us. Where we will live, our standard of living, and the people with whom we will spend our time are often out of our control. When we follow Jesus, we no longer make our decisions based on more money or good schools or cultural amenities or safety if Jesus is leading us in another direction. As we step out in faith, we learn to trust Christ to take care of our needs wherever he leads us. Our goal is not to create heaven on earth. "For here we have no lasting city, but we seek the city that is to come" (Hebrews 13:14). This is the difference that often goes unnoticed between us and Christians who are not called to vocational ministry. We do not work to secure a comfortable future for ourselves here on earth; but our time, energies, and emotions are all spent to secure an eternal future for many in heaven.

Jesus describes our lives this way: "Truly, I say to you, there is no one who has left house or brothers or sisters or mother or father or children or lands, for my sake and for the gospel, who will not receive a hundredfold now in this time, houses and brothers and sisters and mothers and children and lands, with persecutions, and in the age to come eternal life. But many who are first will be last, and the last first" (Mark 10:29–31). I have always found this passage intriguing. Like me, you may have asked yourself just when the "hundredfold" of houses and family and land are going to come your way. The part about "persecutions" we get without any problem. Being a pastor's wife and a missionary gave me a tangible connection with this passage. Josiah and I have experienced the wealth of our Father as we have traveled to many places, slept in many houses, and met many new brothers and sisters, fathers and mothers. Leaving all for the sake of the gospel gave us an unexpected connection with God's work in this world and with our family of faith.

Jesus does not say here that every follower of his is called to leave these things. He did not call every believer to do what Peter and Matthew did. But to those of us he calls to make ourselves last in this world by leaving all to follow him into ministry, he promises a reward in both this life and the next. And when all of God's children are finally gathered and it is time for feasting and celebration at the marriage supper of the Lamb (Revelation 19:9), our scattered family will be reunited. The hundredfold of sisters and brothers, mothers and fathers, that Jesus gave us for leaving all will be there with us. Those we love who belong to Jesus—moms, dads, brothers, sisters, children, grandchildren, et al.—who were left behind for ministry will be with us forever. The moment we see Jesus, we will forget the sacrifices we made to follow him and our momentary troubles in ministry will melt away. I can hardly wait to see him. Together we will join the celebration that we have spent our lives anticipating. It will be amazing.

I look forward to seeing you there.

Timeline

1975—Married

1977–1979—Seminary in Mississippi

1979–1980—Seminary internship in Florida

1980–1981—Seminary in Mississippi

1981–1985—Church planting in central Louisiana

1985–1991—Church planting in south Alabama (October 1991 approved by Serge as a team leader for work in Ireland)

1992–1993—Resign from church, sell house, and raise support for Missions

1993–1996—First missionary term in Ireland

1996–1999—Return home for Josiah to fill transitional roll as U.S. Director of Serge, visit supporters, and raise more support for our return

2000–2005—Return to Ireland (Josiah as field director) where many of our off-island trips occurred

2005–2006—Return to U.S. and report to supporters

2006–2010—Josiah takes job as co-pastor of a church in North Carolina (Barbara once again a pastor's wife)

2011–2012—Sell house and raise support to work with Serge where Josiah will oversee the missionaries and renewal work of Serge

2012—Relocate to the Philadelphia area where Serge is based

Endnotes

1. Francis Brown, S. R. Driver, Charles A. Briggs, *A Hebrew-English Lexicon of the Old Testament* (Oxford: Clarendon Press, 1907).

2. Jane Austen, *Pride and Prejudice* (1813).

3. Samuel Trevor Francis, "O the Deep, Deep Love of Jesus" (1834–1925).

4. John Milton, "On His Blindness," *Oxford Book of English Verse*, (Oxford: Oxford University Press, 1939).

5. Foster the People, "Waste," from *Torches* (Smims Coffee and Tea Music Publishing, BMI, 2010).

6. Bob Dylan, "Everything Is Broken," from *Oh Mercy* (Sony Music Entertainment, 1989).

7. Cab Calloway, "A Chicken Ain't Nothin' but a Bird," from *Are You Hep to the Jive?*, Legacy Series.

8. Joseph Epstein, *Envy: The Seven Deadly Sins* (New York: Oxford University Press and the New York Public Library, 2003).

9. William O. Cushing, "O Safe to the Rock That Is Higher Than I," (1823–1903).

10. *Hello Dolly*, 20th Century Fox, 1969.

11. Serge, *Sonship*, 3rd Edition (Greensboro, NC: New Growth Press, 2013).

12. R. L. Burnside, "It's Bad You Know," from *Come On In* (Fat Possum Records, Oxford, Mississippi).

13. Yoel Kahn, *The Three Blessings: Boundaries, Censorship, and Identity in Jewish Liturgy* (New York: Oxford University Press, 2010), 10, 12, 16.

spiritual renewal
grace through you

Disciples who are motivated and empowered by grace to reach out to a broken world are handmade, not mass-produced. Serge intentionally grows disciples through curriculum, discipleship experiences, and training programs.

Curriculum for Every Stage of Growth

Serge offers grace-based, gospel-centered studies for every stage of the Christian journey. Every level of our materials focuses on essential aspects of how the Spirit transforms and motivates us through the gospel of Jesus Christ.

- 101: The Gospel-Centered Series
  (The Gospel-Centered Life, The Gospel-Centered Community)
- 201: The Gospel Transformation Series
  (Gospel Identity, Gospel Growth, Gospel Love)
- 301: The Sonship Course and Serge Individual Mentoring

Gospel Renewal for You

For over 25 years Serge has been discipling ministry leaders around the world through our Sonship course to help them experience the freedom and joy of having the gospel transform every part of their lives. A personal discipler will help you apply what you are learning to the daily struggles and situations you face, as well as, modeling what a gospel-centered faith looks and feels like.

Training to Help You Disciple Better

Serge's discipler training programs have been refined through our work with thousands of people worldwide to help you gain the biblical understanding and practical wisdom you need to disciple others so they experience substantive, lasting growth in their lives. Available for onsite training or via distance learning, our training programs are ideal for ministry leaders, small group leaders or those seeking to grow in their ability to disciple effectively.

FORMERLY WORLD HARVEST MISSION

Serge **Grace at the Fray**   Visit us online at: www.whm.org/grow

www.newgrowthpress.com

mission
grace through you

At Serge we believe that mission begins through the gospel of Jesus Christ bringing God's grace into the lives of believers. It also sustains us and empowers us to go into different cultures bringing the good news of forgiveness of sins and new life to those whom God is calling to himself.

As a cross-denominational, reformed, sending agency with 200 missionaries on over 25 teams in 5 continents, we are always looking for people who are ready to take the next step in sharing Christ, through:

- **Short-term Teams:** One to two-week trips oriented around serving overseas ministries while equipping the local church for mission.

- **Internships:** Eight-week to nine-month opportunities to learn about missions through serving with our overseas ministry teams

- **Apprenticeships:** Intensive 12–24 month training and ministry opportunities for those discerning their call to cross-cultural ministry

- **Career:** One- to five-year appointments designed to nurture you for a lifetime of ministry

---

FORMERLY WORLD HARVEST MISSION

Serge Grace at the Fray   Visit us online at: www.whm.org/go

www.newgrowthpress.com